RECREATIONS

By the same author

Toynbee Hall: Fifty Years of Social Progress

The Englishman's Holiday: A Social History

Public Relations and American Democracy

A VISUAL HISTORY OF MODERN BRITAIN

EDITED BY PROFESSOR JACK SIMMONS

Recreations

J. A. R. PIMLOTT

ILLUSTRATIONS COLLECTED AND ARRANGED BY
ARTHUR LOCKWOOD

STUDIO VISTA

TO MY DAUGHTER JANE

Designed by Arthur Lockwood

© J. A. R. Pimlott 1968

First published 1968 by Studio Vista Limited
Blue Star House, Highgate Hill, London N19
Distributed in Canada by General Publishing Company Limited
30 Lesmill Road, Don Mills, Ontario

Set in Monotype Baskerville
Printed in Holland by N.V. Drukkerij Koch en Knuttel, Gouda

SBN 289 27698 5

CONTENTS

LIST OF ILLUSTRATIONS

The compiler and publishers are grateful to all those who have supplied photographs and given permission for them to be reproduced. The following abbreviations have been used in the list below: B.M. (illustrations reproduced by courtesy of the Trustees of the British Museum), G.L.C. (Greater London Council), R.T.H.P.L. (Radio Times Hulton Picture Library), V. & A. (Victoria and Albert Museum).

INTRODUCTION

I gladly accepted Professor Simmons' invitation to write this book because like him I felt that recreations have had insufficient attention from historians. It is true that – probably thanks to the influence of G. M. Trevelyan – they nowadays receive a few paragraphs in most general histories, and there is a fairly extensive literature of uneven quality on some of the more specialized aspects such as field sports, cricket and Sunday observance. As far as I know, however, this short essay on a vast subject is the first attempt to deal comprehensively with the history of recreations in Britain in relation to the economic and social background.

What do I mean by 'recreations'? I am tempted to reply that like the elephant they can be readily recognized but less easily defined. One of my difficulties has been the absence of a satisfactory conceptual framework for the systematic study of leisure and recreations. Much illuminating work has been done on this question particularly by Continental and American sociologists but we are not yet in sight of fully coherent definitions of either term – possibly because in the last resort neither is capable of precise definition. It is impossible to make more than crude measurements of the amount of leisure which is available. It is common ground that leisure is 'free time' not pre-empted by work but in assessing the time which is at the individual's free disposal account must be taken of variables such as the time required for other essential activities like eating and resting and bringing up families and for social obligations like the care of aged relatives and the discharge of civic duties. Similarly with recreations. On a strict interpretation what is recreational is determined by the individual's state of mind, and some may find recreation in adult education or archaeology while others prefer football pools or judo. Cricket is undoubtedly a recreation, but does it cease to be recreational when it is compulsory or is played for money or prestige?

In the circumstances any working definition is bound to be arbitrary and some blurring of the edges is inevitable. Broadly I have used the term 'recreations' – almost but not quite synonymously with 'sports and pastimes' – for the kind of things people do when they want to amuse themselves, irrespective of whether the same things are also done for other reasons. But I do not claim to have been consistent, and even within this framework I have had to be highly selective. This has been partly due to limitations of space but mainly because all recreational activities are not equal in historical significance. Contrast, for example, the tournament and table tennis, or chess and snap. I have applied three main tests – the extent to which a recreation was pursued and the importance of the social groups concerned: whether it was especially characteristic of the period: and whether it was an innovation with an important future. I have given priority to the new and evolving over the old and static and to the recreations which have had the widest social repercussions. I have been particularly interested in the tensions which have given rise to social conflict and created political problems. Mainly because they raise largely separate issues, I have for the most part excluded children's recreations, music and the arts and the grosser vices.

If, as is indeed the case, this book is mainly concerned with the recreations of minorities, particularly young males and the upper classes, this reflects the weight of the evidence and the common judgement of their relative social importance through the centuries. By contrast the recreations of the masses – at least until recent times – have chiefly attracted attention when they have brought the participants inot conflict with authority. We are disproportionately well informed about those of their recreations which have met with the disapproval of administrators and magistrates, priests and moralists. But this is also when they made history.

No historical work can be better than its sources, and, as will be evident, there are many points on which authoritative views are impossible in the present state of knowledge. I hope that this book will at least show that holidays and recreations are much more relevant to the main stream of political and economic history than is usually recognized, and that it may stimulate further research and study. I would also like to think that it may be found useful in current discussions about problems of leisure. There is a striking similarity in the problems which recreations have presented to society at different periods in the past and in the steps – so often ineffectual – which those in authority have taken to deal with them. This is a field in which I am sure that history has important lessons to teach.

I am greatly indebted to Professor Simmons for much encouragement and valuable advice. Mr Arthur Lockwood, who has collected and arranged the illustrations, has been an ideal collaborator. I am responsible for the captions. Of others who have helped me I should like in particular to thank my son-in-law, Mr Gordon P. Baker, Fellow of St John's College, Oxford. He has done much to clarify my thinking. And without the London Library this book could scarcely have been written.

Wimbledon, October 1967   J.A.R.P.

I

THE MIDDLE AGES

If leisure is narrowly interpreted as time not devoted to work and other essential activities, most people in the Middle Ages had more leisure than most of their descendants until recent times.*

The medieval system of holidays reflected the conditions of a predominantly agricultural society at a relatively early stage of development. In addition to the weekly holiday on Sunday, there were holidays at significant points in the agricultural calendar, and they were marked by customs which were derived from pagan observances whose original purpose had been to promote the fertility of crops, beasts and men. The main annual holiday was at Christmas when there was little or no work on the land. This was the season when at the turn of the solar year primitive people had most urgently felt the need to propitiate the forces of nature with 'Yule' and other mid-winter festivities. Other substantial periods of holiday occurred at Easter and Whitsun, and there were a varying number of single holidays, mainly on Church festivals.

Not much is known in detail about the extent to which the nominal holidays were observed in practice, but the Twelve Days of Christmas and holidays of about a week at Easter and Whitsun seem normally to have been kept in full in thirteenth and fourteenth-century villages, and work usually stopped on several other holidays which typically included May Day, midsummer and the parish wakes day.[1] The position in the towns was probably similar. Ordinances for building workers in 1474 provided for 37 whole or partial holidays, which were divided into 13 'principal feasts', 15 feasts with vigils and 9 'mean holidays'[2]: holidays with pay were anticipated by the custom of paying wages for alternate festivals in the building trades. Sunday was everywhere a day of recreation, and the modern weekend was foreshadowed by the practice of starting the weekly holiday on Saturday afternoon which was spreading in towns in the later Middle Ages. Work stopped at three or four o'clock, and occasionally even as early as noon in strict accordance with the requirements of the Canon law under which the celebration of a feast began at noon on the vigil.[3] In town and country the recognized holidays were supplemented by other breaks from work for fairs and markets, weddings and funerals, sporting events and public occasions, or without any pretext at all. There were few incentives to sustained hard work. What we should now call absenteeism was prevalent, and time hung heavily in the long winter evenings.

Like the system of holidays medieval recreations showed both pagan and Christian influences and developed within the limits set by the restrictive economic and social conditions. Communications were poor, the majority lived at or below subsistence level, literacy was uncommon, the social hierarchy was rigid, the monetary system was primitive and the division of labour for the most part rudimentary. To an extent

* This is true however elastically the term 'Middle Ages' is defined. In this chapter I have used it broadly for the period between the Norman Conquest and the Reformation and 'the later Middle Ages' for the fourteenth century onwards.

hard to appreciate today medieval people spent their lives in small self-centred groups linked by physical propinquity or occupation, and largely depended for their recreations upon their own cultural and material resources. As G. G. Coulton said, two London buses would hold the adult population of a large medieval village. In 1200 London itself had only about 20,000 inhabitants[4] and in 1500 perhaps about 75,000; the other important towns were much smaller.

Tradition was strong, and conditions were unfavourable to innovation. But, though the rate of change was slow, the situation was never static. Mainly through its close contacts with France, Britain sooner or later imported most of the ideas and techniques which were generated on the Continent or taken over from the Arab world. Recreations also shared in the tendencies towards greater diversification and sophistication which accompanied the gradual dissolution of the traditional social and economic order in the later Middle Ages. Like most present-day holidays, most modern recreations can be traced back to the Middle Ages.

The development of holidays and recreations was also affected by controls imposed by the civil and ecclesiastical authorities. The former were mainly but by no means exclusively concerned with the maintenance of public order. Tournaments were variously banned, licensed and taxed, chiefly because of the risk that they might be a cover for armed insurrection. Brothels and prostitutes were banned and regulated by local authorities as public nuisances and because they were associated with crime. The sale of liquor was controlled. Curfews were enforced because of the danger from criminals in the ill-lit streets, and special care was necessary at holiday-times when they could pass as mummers or revellers. More commonly it was a routine matter of protecting the public against youths who played football in streets and churchyards and of checking the drunken violence into which popular holidaymaking so often degenerated. The first specific reference to football occurs in 1314 when it was banned by the Lord Mayor of London because of the great noise caused in the city by 'hustling over large footballs in the fields of the public.' There were also many examples of intervention for other than police reasons. Sunday observance was regulated by municipalities and gilds, and the Sunday Fairs Act of 1448 – the oldest Sunday observance law still in force – was passed because 'for great earthly covetise' some boroughs refused to close their Sunday markets. The laws relating to hunting and falconry protected ruling class privileges, and the recreations of apprentices were controlled partly at least for their own welfare. Gambling was restricted for economic reasons, for the prevention of crime and because it was a distraction from archery training. In Scotland as well as England defence policy underlay the periodical reenactment of the obligation to practise archery on Sundays and other holidays and the prohibition of football and other 'vain games of no value' which men and boys too often preferred.

The Church was, however, the main agency for policing recreations and for guaranteeing and enforcing what were literally 'holy days'. Officially at least it sought to impose an ideology which was at complete variance from popular tradition and practice. In its most extreme form the Puritanism of the medieval Church was summed up in St John Chrysostom's question: 'Christ is crucified, and dost thou laugh?' The stricter theologians allowed no place for recreations, including physical exercises, except when they were justified on other grounds such as military training or hunting for food: some saw special virtue in physical sickness. The orthodox view of holidays was that they should be wholly devoted to God. Aquinas, who took a relatively liberal view of recreations at other times, did not condone them on holidays. What was later to be called Sabbatarianism was taken for granted by medieval theologians. There were three permissible uses of Sunday, said Wyclif, thinking about God, speaking to God, worshipping God; and the leading English canonist of the age, William Lyndwood, said in the fifteenth century that Sunday should be spent exclusively in hymns and psalms and spiritual songs.

In practice the Church came to terms with reality. Even in ecclesiastical establishments it was forced to tolerate the boy bishop ceremonies at Christmas-time in which young clerks and students reacted against the austerity of the normal regime with licentious and sometimes blasphemous conduct. In practice there was never any question of stopping popular amusements on holidays. Priority had to be given to the difficult task of enforcing attendance at Church services and the observance of holidays as days on which 'servile' work was forbidden. Special vigilance was necessary against the persistence or revival of 'pagan' customs. There was no alternative but to acquiesce in the universal practice under which, after attendance at church, holidays were given up to recreations, and to recognize the fact that many of the clergy joined in. The most that could be done was to condemn – and punish through the penitential and the ecclesiastical courts – the grosser of the extravagances to which human frailty was liable at holiday times. No doubt they were sometimes less lurid than they seemed in clerical eyes. After all, dancing in any form was condemned as an invention of the Devil. But it was sadly true that, as Wyclif said of Christmas, 'gluttony, lechery and all manner of harlotry' were prevalent at holiday seasons. Medieval preachers lamented the regrettable paradox that there was more crime and drunkenness on Sundays than in the rest of the week.

What more than anything else distinguished most medieval from most modern recreations was their communal character. In town and country the traditional holidays were celebrated with rites and ceremonies in which all participated. The village customs were paralleled by the pageantry which developed in corporate bodies such as municipalities, gilds, inns of court and universities: the Lord Mayor's show and livery company banquets are present-day descendants. Much of the ritual went back directly or indirectly to pre-Christian times but new rites continued to evolve. Ritual foods were eaten – the boar's head at Christmas or goose at Martinmas. There were processions to places formerly held sacred. According to one theory the mass football matches between neighbouring villages which were traditional in some areas and still occasionally survive (as at Hallaton and Medbourne in Leicestershire) originated in the scramble for the skull of the sacrificial animal in ancient fertility rites. There were mumming, masking and dancing: they probably played an important part in the Christmas and 'summer games' to which there begin to be references by the thirteenth century. The carol was imported from France in the same period as a song with dance which was not connected with a specific season and only gradually came to be identified with Christmas. Miracle and mystery plays developed with the tolerance and even the sponsorship of the Church. The Robin Hood myth was assimilated into the May Day celebrations. Its origin in popular protest was so far irrelevant by the sixteenth century that Robin Hood and his band attended the Mayings of Henry VIII and entertained him with shooting matches and a collation of venison.

The most important recreational institution was the feast – using the term for the communal eating and drinking which was associated with all medieval holidays and celebrations. The gargantuan feasts which were given by kings and noblemen on special occasions can stand comparison with any in the history of conspicuous consumption. Along with much else, the 6000 guests at the installation of Archbishop Neville of York in 1467 were provided with 300 tuns of ale, 100 tuns of wine, 104 oxen, 1000 sheep, 304 calves, over 500 deer, 2000 pigs, 400 swans, 2000 geese, 1000 capons and over 13,500 birds of other kinds.[5] On the more routine occasion of the bishop of Hereford's Christmas celebrations in 1289 a company of rather over fifty consumed two carcasses and three-quarters of beef, two calves, four does, sixty fowls, eight partridges, two geese, forty-four gallons of wine, and an unmeasured quantity of ale. This was for the three meals on Christmas Day.[6]

Similarly at other levels. The custumal of a manor belonging to the Priory of Tynemouth prescribed that at the Christmas feast there should be different menus according to rank – one hen between two squires, half a hen between two of lesser rank, and 'gross' flesh and cheese for cowherds and their peers. All were to have 'good and proper ale'.[7] Christmas was in a special category but it was only a matter of degree. The legend that the English were more addicted to drunkenness and over-eating than other nations has no surer foundation than a few widely scattered *obiter dicta*, but there is no lack of evidence that they ate and drank hard whenever the opportunity arose. At the other end of the scale were the parties at the taverns on Sundays and other holidays and the 'ales' - at tavern or church hall or private house – which were popular throughout the Middle Ages and were in some cases the only important custom which survived when the traditional holidays began to decline. Sometimes there were music and minstrelsy as well as food and drink. In the later Middle Ages 'ales' were one of the chief methods of raising money for church funds, and they were also devoted to other good causes – such as a wedding present at a 'bride ale', and a whip round for a neighbour in distress at a 'help ale'.[8]

Good eating and drinking have always been recreations in themselves. This was especially true of an age in which the usual diet was monotonous and often sparse. Feasts were also the occasion for music, recitation, dancing, party games and other amusements provided by the company itself. 'Let no man come into this hall', said a sixteenth century Christmas carol, 'but that some sport he bring withal . . . . and if he say he can nought do . . . to the stocks then let him go.'[9]

Proficiency with voice and instrument and mastery of the traditional songs and dances were among the skills which each generation passed on to the next. Only fragments have survived of the medieval repertoire of songs but it was extensive. Some were ancient but certainly in the later Middle Ages many were topical. Often coarse and lewd, they dealt with such immemorial themes as the weaknesses of women and especially wives, the delights and hazards of drink, and money. 'Money, money, thou goest away, and wilt not bide with me.'[10] Instrumental music did not develop in its own right until the fourteenth century: hitherto it had been mainly an accompaniment to song and dance. Popular instruments in the later Middle Ages included the fiddle, the shawm, the pipe and the tabor, and the Welsh were famous as harpists. Dancing was popular everywhere – even in nunneries – in spite of the strictures of the Church. William Fitzstephen told how in twelfth-century London the maidens danced as long as they could see on all the summer holidays, and from later evidence we know how in the villages there would be dancing at the taverns and in the churchyard or round the maypole after service on Sunday and during the summer evenings.

There were always some professional entertainers, and the number grew with increasing wealth and ease of communications. By the thirteenth and fourteenth centuries entertainers from all over the country were flocking to great occasions such as royal weddings: over 400 attended the wedding of Edward I's daughter Margaret. The minstrels – as it is convenient to call the many kinds of entertainer – prospered notwithstanding the official opposition of the Church because rich and powerful people, including bishops, were increasingly prepared to pay for more sophisticated amusements.

Minstrelsy went back to two main sources – the Anglo-Saxon gleemen much as they had existed before the settlement of Britain, and the Norman *joculatores* or *jongleurs* who were ultimately descended from professional entertainers of the late Roman Empire. The two traditions converged after the Norman Conquest.

The public attitude of the Church, though sometimes equivocal, was always hostile. In instructions on the difficult question of how to handle minstrels in the confessional, Thomas de Chabham, sub-dean of Salisbury, told the clergy in about 1300 that all minstrels except those who sang the deeds of princes and the lives of the saints were sure of damnation.[11] Like professional entertainers in all ages the minstrels were undoubtedly a mixed lot. Some were little more than vagabonds. Others like the *joculatores* of William the Conqueror and Henry I were men of considerable wealth and status. There were singers and reciters, dancers, buffoons, contortionists, acrobats, conjurors, stilt-walkers, bear-wards and other animal performers.

The itinerant minstrels were sure of a welcome in the villages and market towns and often in religious houses but the future lay with those who entered the employment of wealthy households and corporate bodies and were the forerunners of the professional actor and musician. In the fourteenth and fifteenth centuries it was common for the households of noblemen (spiritual as well as temporal) and rich merchants to employ companies of musicians and other entertainers, often including a private comedian or 'fool'. Municipalities, gilds and other corporate bodies followed suit. By the fifteenth century many towns had their own companies of 'histriones' or 'waits'. The primary duty of the waits was to sound the watch but they also attended civic functions, played at banquets, gave public performances and took outside engagements. The rising status and increasing professionalism of the minstrels were recognised by Edward IV when he granted a charter for a gild of minstrels in 1469.

Hunting was an economic necessity in the Middle Ages but it was not for this reason that it exercised an almost obsessive fascination over the European aristocracy. Of Alfred it was said that he divided his time between hunting and governing, of Edward the Confessor that he was equally devoted to masses and hunting, and of William the Conqueror that he loved the stags as if he were their father. Hunting, according to *The Master of Game* in the early fifteenth century, contributed to a man's spiritual as well as physical wellbeing. The huntsman eschewed the seven deadly sins, he lived longer than other people, and his life in the woods was a prelude to Paradise.[12] According to the canonist, John of Ayton, on the other hand, hunting for pleasure was a mortal sin, even in a layman.

The techniques, the ritual, the code of conduct, and the language by which hunting as a sport were differentiated from hunting for the sake of meat or skins were largely taken over from France, and as on the Continent the Crown and the aristocracy reserved to themselves a virtual monopoly of the sport in its most favoured forms. The 'beasts of the chase' which were given maximum protection were the red deer, the fallow deer, the wild boar and the roe deer (until full protection was withdrawn from it in the fourteenth century because it drove out other deer). Animals which had limited protection included the hare, the fox, the wild cat and the squirrel. The hare came next in esteem to the stag. 'A good little beast,' said *The Master of Game*, and 'much good sport and much liking to the hunting of her.' The wolf suffered the reverse of protection: rewards were offered for its extermination. The rabbit was not known in Britain until the thirteenth century and did not become plentiful until the fifteenth.[13]

The effect of the forest laws and of the game laws which began to replace them in the fourteenth century was to deny to all but a small minority the opportunity of hunting lawfully even on their own land. The social cost was high. Land needed for agricultural development was sterilized, the burden of administration was heavy, and poor people were forbidden access to large areas not only to hunt for food but to collect firewood and feed their pigs. Serious tension was caused, and poaching – chiefly no doubt for food rather than simply for sport – was widespread, even among the clergy. The rebels of 1381 demanded free hunting and fishing, and the poacher Robin Hood became a folk hero. But the main objects of the policy were achieved, and, though not conceived in these terms, the restrictions were essential on conservationist grounds if the sport was to survive. Too many hunters chasing fewer game as agriculture encroached on the hunting grounds could only lead to the extinction of the beasts which were essential to its pursuit as a source of food and skins as well as for pleasure. Even with protection the wild boar had largely died out by the thirteenth century.

The ancient and curious sport of hawking, or falconry, was known in China in 2000 B.C. and probably reached England through France in the ninth century. Harold was a keen falconer. Hawking was costly, it was a severe test of skill and endurance, it was protected by law, and it ranked with hunting in the favour of kings and noblemen. The Emperor Frederick II's classic *De Arte Venandi cum Avibus* was read throughout Europe, the Crusades grave a new impetus to the sport, and falconers imported birds from the East as well as the Continent, especially Norway.

Fishing was important as a source of food: the monk fishing for his Friday dinner is part of the popular stereotype of medieval Britain. But it was also well developed as a sport, and from the earliest English book on the subject, a small treatise *On fysshinge with an angle*, we know that artificial flies were in use by the fifteenth century.

Like hunting the tournament originated in a practical need and developed into a sport for its own sake. It began as a stage in the education and training of young men of high birth for the profession of arms. As it changed its character it developed rules, rituals and techniques which were of diminishing relevance to warfare. It was a test of the physical prowess and other qualities which were expected of every gentleman. It became a social event in which women took an important part, and a spectator sport for all classes.

When the tournament came to England in the twelfth century – almost certainly from France – the main feature was the *mêlée* fought by groups of horsemen over open country. The conditions were so realistic that an actual battle sometimes developed – as happened when the Northern met the Southern Knights in 1236 and the Papal Legate was called in to mediate. 'A sport which they call a tournament,' wrote a witty monk, 'but the better name would be torment.' By the fourteenth century the main item was the joust in which one competitor rode against another with the object of dismounting him or breaking his lance. Other forms of single combat were included, ceremonial had been introduced, and the tournament ended with feasting, minstrelsy and dance. Though always dangerous the sport was humanised by the use of blunted weapons and by insistence on strict rules of conduct. Special arenas were built with stands for spectators: large crowds attended the main London tournament ground at Smithfields. The rules governing the sport were codified by John Tiptoft, Earl of Worcester, in the name of Edward IV. But by this time it was already doomed. With the introduction of plate armour the weight of metal on man and horse grew heavier, and the development of specialized armour for tournament use in the fourteenth century both added to the cost of taking part and further diminished its relevance to the practice of war. The decline of chivalry and economic pressures on the lesser land-lords reduced its appeal, and the loss of speed and manoeuvrability as the weight of armour increased made it less attractive as a sport and a spectacle. Tilting contin-ued to be popular but by the sixteenth century the tournament as such had degene-rated into little more than a pageant.

It was not only on the tournament ground that, in an age when organized violence and war were endemic, sports were practised which mimicked battle and were rele-vant to war. In the later Middle Ages country houses had their tilts at which the owner and his sons exercised with horse and lance. From six years to sixty able-bodied males were bound by law to train with the bow, and every community of any size had its archery butts. As the Act of 1471 said, 'Every person mighty and able should have his bow, because that the defence of this land standeth much by archers'. And in spite of the disorder and bloodshed which they too often caused the authorities looked with favour on other manly sports such as leaping, running, wrestling and swimming which fitted young men for military service.

William Fitzstephen gave a vivid picture of the popular sports in his famous de-scription of twelfth-century London. Similar scenes – differing only in scale and detail – could have been witnessed throughout the country, and John Stow said that it was still applicable in the sixteenth century. Every Friday in Lent companies of young men with lances and shields practised 'feats of war' in the presence of members of the Court and leading citizens. In the Easter holidays battles were fought on the Thames. Young men in boats without oars tilted against shields hung upon poles fixed in midstream, and the crowds upon the riverside laughed at those who toppled into the water. On holidays during the summer the young men were 'exercised in leaping, dancing, shooting, wrestling, casting the stone, and practising their shields'; and when the 'great fen' at Moorfields froze in winter they would charge one another with poles. Some broke their legs, some their arms, but 'youth desirous of glory in this sense exercised itself against the time of war.'

Fitzstephen also told how the London schoolboys were introduced to the always popular blood sports, which were probably of pre-Christian origin. Every Shrove Tuesday they 'delighted themselves in cock-fighting'. In the winter bulls and bears were baited, and boars were set to fight. The popularity of football in both England and Scotland is shown by the number of references – usually in the form of prohibitions and records of inquests and other Court proceedings. Little is known in detail about the medieval game but by common consent it was, as Sir Thomas Elyot said in 1531, nothing but 'beastly fury and extreme violence'.* With few if any rules and no referee it was a constant threat to public order, and, apart from being a distraction from archery, this was presumably why it was regarded with such disfavour by responsible people. In Scotland golf, which may have originated in the Netherlands, was played by all ranks. Its prohibition along with football in the fifteenth century seems to have been as ineffectual as similar prohibitions on similar grounds in England. James IV, who also played football, bought his golf-clubs from a Perth bow-maker. Other sports of which little is known except that they were popular enough to be banned from time to time included bowls (known in England by the thirteenth century), skittles, quoits, club-ball (which may have been an ancester of cricket), the hurling of stones, and tennis (an importation from France).

The national passion for gambling was well developed. Wagers were laid on any pretext, including most sports. Dice, probably the oldest form of gambling, was played universally – in the home, at taverns, in monasteries and colleges, at night spots where (as described by Chaucer) 'young folk that haunted folly with harps, lutes and gitterns dance and play at dice both day and night.' The chief indoor games – 'tables', cards and chess – were all played for money. 'Tables' was the collective name for the race games of ancient origin which were played on the backgammon board: eight varieties were mentioned in England in 1300. Cards, which probably originated in Asia, quickly became popular after their introduction from France probably in the late fourteenth century; late medieval costumes are still depicted on modern Court cards. All 'loud disports' ceased when the Paston household was in mourning in 1483, but there was 'playing at the tables, and the chess, and cards.'

Chess is of special interest as the indoor game which shared with hunting and the tournament in the special affection of noblemen and kings. Noteworthy royal addicts included John, Edward I and Henry VI of England and James I and James IV of Scotland: John is said to have played chess when he should have been relieving Rouen. It originated in India, was imported into Europe probably through the Moors in Spain, was probably first played outside Spain by the tenth century, and was known in England soon after the Conquest. Medieval chess differed from the modern game mainly in the relative weakness of the queen and the bishop, and it did not take its modern form until late in the fifteenth century when the value of the queen was increased more than fivefold and the bishop's nearly threefold. These changes originated in southern Europe but we know neither to whose genius they were due, the reasons which prompted them, nor by what process of international agreement they came into general use. Were the reasons technical, springing from the logic of the game and the desire to perfect it? In a game which was ultimately based on war and politics were they consciously or unconsciously related to changes in the political and social structure? Was it coincidental that they occurred in the period which is usually regarded as the bridge between the medieval and modern world, and why is it that the rules have been so little changed since?

* 'Biting and "putting in the boot" are the most vicious and detestable symptoms of dangerous play that has become far too common in Rugby Union.' (*Sunday Times*, 30 Oct. 1966)

AFTER THE REFORMATION

It is convenient to start a new chapter with the Reformation, but it would be mislead-ing to give the impression that the religious changes were the main cause of the developments in the field of recreations which came to a bizarre climax during the Puritan ascendancy. Almost everything that happened can be traced to trends already discernible in the Middle Ages and the spread of the new religious ideas was only a contributory factor in the most important change. This was the wide-spread adoption of puritanical attitudes which had hitherto been confined to a minority of priests and monks and seldom translated into practice even by them.

The crisis was not in any case reached until the seventeenth century. Superficially the position changed little at first. Under Humanist influence, it is true, responsible men could now express openly a more balanced view of recreations, and within limits pleasure was acceptable as an end in itself. Sir Thomas Elyot was at great pains in *The Governor* to prove that St. Augustine had not condemned every form of dancing and that properly used it had positive moral virtues. With the rediscovery of Galen the value of exercise to health was recognised, and for the first time since the Ancient World physical recreation needed no extraneous justification. The zest for sport exemplified by Henry VIII was not exceeded until the public-school revolution in the nineteenth century.

Ideas such as these were given wide currency in the many books on the upbringing of gentlemen (often of girls as well) which were popular in the sixteenth century. Sir Thomas Elyot stressed the development of the whole man. Roger Ascham, perhaps the greatest educationist of his time, recommended that boys should be given a comprehensive introduction to suitable sports and pastimes. 'To ride comely,' he wrote in *The Schoolmaster* (1570), 'to run fair at the tilt or ring, to play at all weapons, to shoot fair in bow or surely in gun, to vault lustily; to run, to leap, to wrestle, to swim; to dance comely, to sing and play of instruments cunningly; to hawk, to hunt, to play at tennis and all pastimes generally, which be joined with labour, used in open place and in the daylight, containing either some fit exercise for war, or some pleasant pastime for peace, be not only comely and decent, but also very necessary for a courtly gentleman to use.' In the *Anatomy of Melancholy* (1621) Robert Burton gave an unsur-passed analysis of the case for almost every form of recreation if practised in moder-ation.

The contrast with medieval orthodoxy could hardly be more striking. The diffe-rence was less important in practice. The correlation between actual conduct and the medieval code of ethics had been slight, and Ascham's cautiously expressed pro-gramme contained little which had not in essence been part of the conventional education of young men of good birth in the age of chivalry. What is more, medieval asceticism continued to influence even Humanist writers, and a distinction was drawn between what was fitting for the 'courtly' and for other classes. With the eccentric exception of Richard Mulcaster, Tudor schoolmasters had little time for sport and other recreations among their pupils. And the Reformation scarcely interrupted the continuity of official policy. Under Thomas Cromwell and Cranmer the number of holidays was somewhat reduced because, said the Order of 1536, they were the occasion of much 'sloth and idleness, riot and superfluity'. But some of the traditional holidays had been falling into disuse, and the provision which was made in the Holy Days and Fasting Days Act of 1551 was medieval in doctrine and cannot have been far out of line with late medieval practice. In addition to Sundays it prescribed 27 holidays, including six at Christmas and two at Easter and Whitsun. Holidays were 'days on which Christians should cease from all other kinds of labours and should apply themselves only and wholly to the holy works properly pertaining unto true religion.' The Act was also characteristically medieval in the equivocation with which it dealt with enforcement. Failure to observe it was to be punished by the censures of the Church and appropriate penance could be imposed. Yet anybody at his 'free will and pleasure' could work on holidays when necessity should require.

Nor were there any changes in the pattern of recreations which could not more obviously be attributed to social and technological developments than to changing attitudes towards the use of leisure. The many sports mentioned by Burton in the *Anatomy of Melancholy* included few if any which had not been known in the Middle Ages. Horse racing, wild goose chases, riding the great horse, tilts and tournaments were among the sports of greater men, along with the traditional field sports which in Burton's opinion took up too much of their time. Each was objectively discussed but in the Renaissance spirit Burton specially commended study and excursions 'to visit friends, see cities, castles, towns.' In a long list of recreations common among country folk he mentioned ninepins, quoits, pitching of bars, hurling, wrestling, leaping, running, fencing, swimming, cudgel play, foils, football and quintain. Winter amusements included cards, tables, dice, chess, the philosopher's game (a variant of chess), shuttlecock, billiards, music, masques, singing, dancing, Yule games, frolics, jests, riddles, catches, purposes, questions and commands, and 'merry tales, which some delight to hear, some to tell.'

As a major institution the tournament spent itself at the Field of Cloth of Gold in 1521, but jousting and tilting retained their popularity. Like many of her subjects Elizabeth loved the tilt more even than tennis, it was said. None the less it was becoming a romantic irrelevance, and 'tilting breathed its last when King Charles left London,' wrote John Aubrey. The fate of archery was to be similar. Henry VIII was an expert bowman and a patron of archers; and the Act of 1541 'for the maintenance of artillery and the debarring of unlawful games' restated the ancient obligations to practise archery. Roger Ascham's *Toxophilus*, the first English work on archery, was published in 1545, and a third of the levies raised to meet the Armada were bowmen. In 1583 as many as 3,000 archers took part in one of the innumerable archery meetings and pageants. But whether for war, in hunting or as a sport for its own sake archery could not long withstand the spread of firearms. In 1595 it was decided that bows and arrows should no longer be kept as munitions of war, and with the invention of more practical firearms such as the calliver they were doomed in the hunting field. It was in vain that James I and Charles I tried to stop encroachments on the London archery grounds and that the bowmen appealed for governmental action to arrest the decay of their ancient craft. As a pastime archery survived the civil war – Charles II was a keen archer – but even as a sport it was gradually to die out.

Ascham contrasted the neglect of archery with the rise of fencing, which met the needs of self-defence as well as being practised as a sport. It was encouraged by Henry VIII, and the foreign weapons and methods which spread in the second half of the century flourished despite opposition from those who took the attractive but short-sighted view that the traditional sword and buckler were good enough for Englishmen. By 1600 there were many fencing schools, the more practical Italian techniques had prevailed over the 'Euclidean' style of the Spaniards, the sword and buckler had been largely relegated to serving men, and the dagger and the rapier were the weapons of gentlemen.

Nothing challenged the pre-eminence of hunting – least of all the mutterings of extreme Puritans such as Philip Stubbes, and the faint beginnings of a humanitarian revolt against blood sports. Elizabeth rode to hounds until she was an old woman, and James I's Court complained that he was too fond of the sport. Neither in or out of Christendom, Andrew Boorde had written in the 1540s after extensive foreign travel, had he found so much pleasure for 'hart and hind, buck and doe, and for roebuck and doe as in England.' The stag was still king of the chase, poaching was widespread and reputable, and the hare (which was coursed as well as hunted) was the most popular quarry. 'The timorous flying hare,' wrote Shakespeare, 'how he outruns the winds, and with what care he cranks and courses with a thousand doubles.'

Isaak Walton's *Compleat Angler or The Contemplative Man's Recreation* (1653) is the most famous of several books which express the fascination of fishing for Tudor and Stuart England. Henry Peacham in 1622 called it 'the honest and patient man's recreation'. Many gentlemen, said Robert Burton, 'will wade up to the arm-holes and voluntarily undertake that, to satisfy their pleasure, which a poor man would scarce be hired to undergo.'

It was the last great age in the history of falconry – three important books on the subject were published between 1575 and 1620 – but while like archery it was threatened by the improvements in sporting firearms its decline did not become obvious until the Restoration when many who had closed their mews during the Civil War did not reopen them. Burton looked upon shooting as a form of 'fowling'. Fowling, he said, was 'delightsome to some sorts of men, be it with guns, lime, nets, glades, gins, strings, baits, pit-falls, pipes, calls, stalking-horses, setting-dogs, coy-ducks, etc., or otherwise.'

The status of football remained as ambiguous as ever. The cause of many conflicts with the authorities, it was additionally offensive to the Puritans because of its popularity on Sundays, and that it was not confined to the lower classes is shown by the need for James I to advise his son that it was 'a laming exercise not to be used by a prince'. For once Stubbes expressed the general view when he described it as a 'bloody and murdering practice,' and Richard Mulcaster, successively headmaster of Merchant Taylors and St. Paul's, was exceptional in seeing the better side. As he said in 1581, football would not have grown to 'the greatness that it is now at if it had not had great helps both to health and strength.' To counteract its barbarous tendencies he proposed limitations on the number of players and – with even deeper insight – the appointment of training masters who would act as coach and referee.

Bowls was probably the most popular sport: of the images which Shakespeare drew from games, it accounted for over three times as many as any other.[14] Bias had already been given to the bowls, it demanded high skill, but its attractiveness was mainly as a vehicle for gambling. Other important gambling media were dice, cards, tables, cock-fighting, bear-baiting and tennis. Young children were given money with which to play, and educationists did not object to gambling in moderation. After all there were worse ways of passing the time. As Ascham said – speaking from personal experience as an inveterate and unsuccessful gambler – 'a man should never slay another with shooting wide at the cards.' Cheating had long been well developed and was taken for granted: a book published in 1608 listed fourteen kinds of false dice, and Ben Jonson said that Queen Elizabeth always played with loaded dice.

Other vices also luxuriated particularly in London, by 1600 a cosmopolitan capital with perhaps 300,000 inhabitants. Shakespeare has immortalized the denizens of the Elizabethan tavern. 'Some men's delight,' wrote Burton, 'is to take tobacco, and drink all day long in a tavern or ale-house, to discourse, sing, jest, roar, talk of a cock and bull over a pot etc.' Prostitution and obscene publications flourished. Violence was endemic. This was one side of the picture. It was also a period which was remarkable not only for supreme achievement in music and drama but for the high level of popular participation in them. Of Elizabethan music, G. M. Trevelyan said lyrically that 'it was a form taken in England by the free, joyful spirit of the Renaissance' and 'the whole country was filled with men and women singing songs, composing the music and writing the verses.' The impression which was made on contemporaries was sometimes less ecstatic. London, wrote Stephen Gosson in the 1570s, was 'so full of unprofitable pipers and fiddlers, that a person can no sooner enter a tavern, than two or three out of them are hard at his heels, to give him a dance before he depart.'

The Elizabethan drama had crystallised from the miracles and mysteries, 'games' and 'plays', mummings and disguisings, interludes, pageants and pastorals of the later Middle Ages and the early Tudor period. 'Methinks,' said a character in *The Winter's Tale*, 'I play as I have seen them do in Whitsun pastorals.' The actors were descended from the minstrels, and the law provided that like other entertainers they were to be treated as rogues and vagabonds unless licensed by the justices. They were forced for their own protection to seek the patronage of great personages who could provide the necessary social and financial backing, and with its wealth and population London provided audiences capable of commercial exploitation. There were many difficulties – due to plague and fire, censorship, internal dissensions, anxious administrators, Puritans – but for the time being a more or less regular audience drawn from all social levels was built up. A corps of first-class playwrights and actors developed. Burbage and other famous London players were forerunners of the modern star, touring companies opened up the provinces, amateur dramatics were stimulated. Fortunes were made by those who like Shakespeare combined talent, luck, an aptitude for business, and sensitivity to popular taste.

This was the crux. The theatre was in the last resort the creature of the audiences, and it was in direct competition with the already entrenched blood sports, especially bull and bear baiting, which had long been organised commercially. Erasmus commented in 1506 on the many herds of bears for baiting he saw in England, and the amphitheatre for bull and bear baiting which was built at Southwark under Henry VIII's patronage in 1526 had about a thousand seats; a second arena was built in about 1570. These spectacles were attended by people of all classes, they gratified the love of gambling as well as the appetite for blood and excitement, and leading theatrical managers also promoted baiting matches. Champion bears were household names and betting was heavy. The first regular cockpit was built by Henry VIII and there were numerous successors. James I experimented unsuccessfully with the baiting of lions. Supporters of bear-baiting defended it against Puritan criticism on the ground that it was a safeguard against worse things. This may not have been without substance. Evidently the blood sports satisfied prevalent psychological needs, and they had their counterpart in the violence which was depicted on the stage. In a violent age aggressive impulses often found more dangerous outlets.

It is still hard to explain satisfactorily the triumph of the puritanical ideas which have so decisively influenced the subsequent history of recreations in Britain. They were not original. Even the wilder Puritans advocated nothing with which medieval theologians would have disagreed, and in this field the moderate Puritans had the support of many who were otherwise out of sympathy with them. What was new was not the ideology but its widespread adoption as a working guide to public policy and private practice. This was without previous parallel. Other Protestants outside Britain and the American colonies seldom went so far, and the comparative ease with which restrictions on traditional amusements were imposed on a pleasure-loving and turbulent people under the successive Puritan régimes remains somewhat of a mystery. As Ralph Josselin said of Londoners in 1646, while they hankered after 'the sports and pastimes that they were wonted to enjoy' it was not long before they were 'in many families weaned from them.'

One reason was that serious-minded people of different political and religious views reacted similarly against excesses which were shocking to their moral sense and were a social threat to public order and economic discipline. James I's Court was notorious for profligacy and vice, and Lawrence Stone's study of the aristocracy has led him to the conclusion that there was a startling increase in extravagance, licence and irresponsibility between 1580 and 1620. Gambling in particular was 'turning from an innocent amusement into a social scourge.' There is no reason to doubt that the same trends operated among all classes: and standards of conduct had scarcely been high before the degeneracy set in.

Deeper causes lay in the disturbance caused to traditional ways by economic and social changes, such as the rise of industry, the extension of a money economy and the great inflation, agricultural depopulation, and the explosive growth of London. Horizons were widened, life even in the country became less self-centred and isolated, new attitudes to work were required and the old holiday customs were of diminishing relevance.

At first the consequences for holidays and recreations were not cataclysmic. The old customs were widely kept up. Throughout the reign of Elizabeth there were complaints that in some areas people were still observing holidays which had been suppressed at the Reformation. Probably in most areas Sunday, as a preacher at Blandford said in 1570, was still the 'revelling day' of the 'multitude' and 'spent in bull-baitings, bear-baitings, bowlings, dicing, carding, dancing, drunkenness and whoredom.'[15] Church ales were a constant source of anxiety to those responsible for law and order. The maypoles were a focus of tension between populace and Puritans, for whom they were linked with paganism, popery and debauchery. The assumption on which James I's *Book of Sports* of 1618 was based was that it was normal for Sundays and other holidays to be devoted to 'lawful and harmless' recreations such as dancing, archery, leaping, vaulting, May games, Whitsun ales and morris dances. This is much the same mixture as in the later Middle Ages. The same impression is given by Puritan propagandists and by Thomas Tusser and other writers about rural life. Sir Thomas Overbury wrote in 1615 of the franklin who allowed 'honest pastime', and without holding them to be relics of Popery kept 'Rock Monday, and the Wake in summer, shroving, the wakeful ketches on Christmas Eve, the Hoky, or Seed Cake' and thought none the worse of it 'though the country lasses dance in the churchyard after Evensong.' Except in detail the picture which Herrick gave of rural holiday-making even later – presumably after taking up his Devonshire living in 1630 – could have just as well applied to the fifteenth century.

> For Sports, for Pagentrie, and Playes,
> Thou hast thy Eves, and Holydayes;
> On which the young men and maids meet,
> To exercise their dancing feet;
> Tripping the comely country round,
> With Daffodils and Daisies crown'd.
> Thy Wakes, thy quintels, here thou hast,
> Thy May-poles too with Garlands grac't:
> Thy Morris-Dance; thy Whitsun-ale;
> Thy Sheering-feast, which never faile.
> Thy Harvest home; thy Wassaile bowle,
> That's tost up after Fox i' th'Hole.
> Thy Mummeries; thy Twelfe-tide Kings
> And Queenes; thy Christmas revellings.

It is also clear that the traditional customs were in decline. Tusser's injunction in 1557, 'old customs that good be, let no man despise,' carried the implication that they were sometimes neglected, and though still of major importance, the greatest of the medieval holidays, Christmas, was itself beginning to wane. 'Oh Christmas, old reverend Christmas.' exclaimed Thomas Taylor the 'Water Poet' in *The Complaint of Christmas* (1631), 'Now it is decayed, ruined, sunk.' Too much significance must not be attached to these and many similar lamentations about the fate of the old Christmas. Christmas still had a strong emotional appeal which it was worth cultivating for propagandist purposes. But we also know of the difficulty which Elizabeth and James I experienced in persuading landlords to leave London in order to keep the traditional Christmas on their estates, and the second half of the sixteenth century saw the almost total disappearance of the elaborate rites with which it had formerly been celebrated at the Court, the inns of court and the universities.

Stronger evidence about changing attitudes to the old holidays is provided by the spread of Sabbatarianism – comprehensively expounded in Nicholas Bownde's *The True Doctrine of the Sabbath* in 1595. This cannot be adequately explained in doctrinal terms. According to Christopher Hill it was ultimately due to the incompatibility of the medieval system of holidays with new economic needs which required an ideology fostering regular working habits. Opposition to the traditional ways of observing Sundays and other holidays came from employers, irrespective of political and religious sympathies, who were affected by the absenteeism and loss of efficiency to which they led. It was commonly associated with a desire to cut down the number of saints' days and other holidays which encouraged idleness and constantly and erratically interrupted industry and trade. Thomas Mun was expressing a widely held view (though by no means unique to this period) when he said in the 1620s that our weak competitive position in international trade was due to 'the general leprosy of our piping, potting, feasting, factions and misspending of our time in idleness and pleasure.'[16] These opinions were widely shared by 'the industrious sort of people' – yeomen, artisans, the smaller merchants and traders – who could ill afford the loss of earnings on holidays yet were anxious that Sunday should be respected as a day of rest from work, free from demoralising amusements and devoted to spiritual improvement. Support for the traditional customs came mainly from the areas – especially in the North and the West – where there had been least economic and social change. The case did not rest solely on conservatism and antagonism to the Puritans. What we should now regard as the main point was stated cogently in the second *Book of Sports* in 1633. 'The meaner sort who labour hard all the week' needed Sunday amusements to refresh their spirits. In effect, to deny them recreations on holidays was to deny them recreations altogether.

Though much confused by other considerations Sabbatarianism was the main issue which underlay the controversy over the *Book of Sports*. The immediate occasion for its publication was a decision of the Lancashire magistrates in 1616 that lawful as well as unlawful pastimes should be forbidden on Sundays and other holidays. James I and his advisers took the opportunity of protests from the county to make a national statement of policy. The *Book of Sports* of 1618 instructed all concerned to allow the pursuit of lawful and harmless recreations after divine service. But it also emphasised that there must be no 'impediment or neglect of divine service' and that unlawful games must not be permitted.

This was entirely orthodox, and by earlier standards it was commonplace and unprovocative. But in the circumstances of the time it was a gesture of resistance to the spread of Sabbatarianism. James I left it at that. He did little or nothing to enforce the *Book of Sports*, but it was reissued in 1633 by Charles I and Laud, and it was due to them that it became a touchstone of loyalty to Church and Crown. Some 800 clergy who refused to read it were ejected from their livings. Ten years later it was cited in Laud's indictment, and the Long Parliament ordered it to be burned. The amount of sympathy with the Puritans on the need to restrict holidays and recreations is shown by the totalitarian sweep of the measures they were able to impose without much difficulty for nearly twenty years. Plays and bear-baiting were banned in 1642, the *Book of Sports* was burned in 1643, and in 1644 the maypoles – symbols of the old order and standing invitations to the irresolute – were ordered to be pulled down, and all trading, sports and games on Sundays were forbidden. Cock-fighting and horse-racing were banned later, and the laws relating to drunkenness and gambling were strengthened. Feast days were suppressed, and Christmas came under special attack. The Puritans, said a Royalist pamphleteer, 'took power and authority to plunder pottage-pots, to ransack ovens, and to strip spits stark naked.'[18]

There were some fluctuations in policy, and the law was not always rigorously enforced. In some rural areas the old ways continued, and Christmas geese continued to be roasted behind closed shutters in the towns. Nor did the prohibitions extend to all recreations, and after the abolition of holidays Parliament provided in 1647 for the second Tuesday in every month to be a day of recreation and relaxation for scholars, apprentices and servants in substitution for the former saints' days. No objection was taken to sport as such. Cromwell was a music lover, and dancing was tolerated: *The English Dancing Master*, which became a standard manual on country dancing, was published in 1651. There were a few demonstrations against the restrictions. Lives were lost at Ipswich and skulls were broken at Oxford in riots caused by the proscription of Christmas in 1647. There was much anger at pettifogging interference with harmless pursuits. But the general impression is of resignation and even acquiescence in the broad objects of the regime, and especially the insistence on strict Sunday observance.

3
AFTER THE RESTORATION

The official view of the Restoration was symbolised by the giant maypole which was set up in the Strand under the personal supervision of the Duke of York and by the morris dancers who welcomed Charles II on his journey from Dover to London. The theatres reopened, bear-baiting was restored, and Englishmen could once again enjoy the roasted pullets, the 'brave plum-porridge' and the mince-pies with which like Samuel Pepys in 1661 they consummated their Christmas celebrations.

In more fundamental matters it was impossible to go back. Especially in the towns the traditional holidays continued to decline. Less and less is heard of the ancient holiday customs except as nostalgic remembrances of the past. Christmas, the *London Magazine* said in 1754, was 'held sacred by good eating and drinking,' and there was not much else to it. The old holidays, said Washington Irving in 1818, resembled 'those picturesque morsels of Gothic architecture which we see crumbling in various parts of the country'.

By a strange irony the Puritan Sabbath became part of the British way of life. It was often imperfectly observed in practice but it was taken for granted in principle by Anglicans and unbelievers as well as by the Dissenters and by the Presbyterians in Scotland. Foreigners noted with amazed interest the curious phenomenon of the English Sunday. Its strict observance, said a visitor to London in 1710, was 'the only point in which one sees that the English profess to be Christians; certainly from the rest of their conduct one would not suspect it of many of them'.[18] Sunday travel – which was forbidden under the Sunday Observance Acts of 1625 and 1675 – was frowned upon in the eighteenth century: some people made Sabbath journeys on the excuse that the highwaymen spent their Sundays at home. Plays, and public music and dancing on Sundays were banned, and Sunday trading was restricted in practice as well as by law. But people were not prevented from enjoying themselves in private, or in the taverns and tea-gardens. In 1760 Sabbath skaters were warned off the canals in St James's Park during hours of divine service with the threat of a press gang which would draft them 'to serve their country against the French' upon 'the frozen lakes of Canada'.[19] The implication is that they could skate at other hours. But notwithstanding the exceptions, foreign opinion was pretty unanimous. 'Is anything in the world so wearisome as the English Sunday?', asked a young Frenchman, François de la Rochefoucauld, in 1784.

Except in Scotland the latent Puritanism was, however, in most other respects less obvious than self-indulgence and laxity. The most characteristic recreations were sociable, and they were usually centred on eating and drinking, and often associated with gambling. The innumerable taverns and inns were universal meeting places for business and pleasure and even the Dissenters frequented them in an age when ale was still the staple drink. 'There is nothing yet contrived by man', said Samuel Johnson, 'by which so much happiness is given as by a good tavern or inn', and the sensible practice under which the customers segregated themselves in separate rooms according to social level made for greater sociability. The coffee and chocolate houses which sprang up after the Restoration performed a similar function. After the prohibition of public gambling in the middle of the century some of them grew into clubs of the modern West End type. White's chocolate house in St. James's was the first to make the transition in the 1750s. Less formal clubs met at the taverns. Johnson's London had clubs for journalists and writers and for many other specialised interests such as politics, debating, sailing, bull-baiting and lotteries: apprentices and prostitutes congregated at the 'cock and hen' clubs. The newly developing friendly societies often had a convivial as well as a practical side. Among the poorer classes the public houses served as social clubs. They were not merely places for drinking but usually the main centres of amusement in the villages and the poorer districts of the towns.

In the country towns the leading inns and taverns were used for dinners and dances, concerts, theatrical performances by touring companies, and 'assemblies' – the not very precise term which was used for many kinds of public social gathering. Assemblies, wrote Daniel Defoe in the 1720s, were 'seminaries of crime', and the chief activities were 'dancing, gaming, intrigues'. Much in fact depended on the organisers. At Bath, where one of the earliest permanent assembly rooms was built in 1708, Richard Nash, the Master of Ceremonies, enforced strict rules of good behaviour which were widely copied elsewhere. When assemblies were introduced into Edinburgh in the 1720s local anxieties were assuaged by arranging for them to be supervised by discreet and formidable matrons whom everybody had to obey. This effectively disposed of the opposition from what Robert Chambers called 'the square-toed part of society.'[21]

Parties at the homes of friends were a favourite form of entertainment. As Defoe pointed out, they had the advantage that good company and excellent conversation could be enjoyed without the usual 'mixture of assemblies, gaming houses, and public foundations of vice and debauchery'. It was not of course as simple as that. Some saw insidious dangers in the seeming innocence of the tea parties (often in the late evening) which became increasingly popular in the eighteenth century. Tea-drinking, Cobbett later maintained, was 'a destroyer of health, an enfeebler of effeminacy and laziness, a debaucher of youth, and a maker of misery for old age'.

On Sundays and summer evenings large numbers of middle and lower class people made use of the many tea gardens and other pleasure resorts in the neighbourhood of London and other towns. They were often run by taverns and often associated with spas, and they flourished in rural retreats such as Dulwich and Streatham, Hampstead and Islington. Nearer the heart of London were the famous pleasure gardens of Ranelagh and Vauxhall: Vauxhall was the livelier but the world of fashion preferred Ranelagh.

Life at the fashionable spas was a variation on the same theme. It was 'but London life on another stage', wrote Elizabeth Montagu of Bath in 1754. The practice of going to spas for medical reasons began to spread in the late sixteenth century but it was not long before the main reason for visiting them was the pursuit of pleasure in a different environment. Of Bath it was said in 1697 that many people of fashion came 'solely to amuse themselves in good company. There are music, play, promenades, balls, and perpetual amusement.'[21] Thanks largely to the organising ability of Richard Nash, Bath became the model for the many other spas which were frequented by the leisured classes. The social homogeneity of the visitors was essential to the way of life. They spent most of their time in company, and they followed a routine under which certain hours were assigned to taking the waters, others to promenades, and others to assemblies. 'The course of things,' said a magazine in 1737, 'is as mechanical as if it went by clockwork.'[22]

The same was at first true of the new holiday resorts on the coast which began to be fashionable in the middle of the eighteenth century. The discovery of the seaside was an obvious sequel to the popularity of the spas. Already in the previous century physicians had recommended sea-water bathing and the drinking of sea-water, and by the 1730s a regular sea-bathing season had been established at the northern spa of Scarborough and the south coast was attracting a few visitors for sea bathing. The rush into the sea which followed in the sixties and seventies has traditionally been ascribed to Dr. Richard Russell's well-timed *Dissertation on the Use of Sea Water in the Diseases of the Glands* (1752). It was ultimately due to deeper causes. The sea and the mountains had hitherto been regarded with revulsion or indifference, and the discovery of the seaside was contemporaneous with the awakening of interest in the wilder aspects of nature which brought the first awestruck tourists to the mountainous districts at home and abroad. The faint beginnings were felt of the 'undescribable emotions' which the sea was to evoke in Sir Edward Denham in Jane Austen's *Sanditon* and which so stirred Charlotte Brontë that she broke down in tears when she first saw it at Bridlington in 1839.

It was inevitable that once discovered the seaside resorts should supplant the spas as the main holiday resorts. The capacity of the coast was almost unlimited, and unlike the spas it was capable of absorbing first in thousands and then in millions the middle and working class visitors who followed the people of fashion as communications and living standards improved. It was quickly discovered that the beach was an ideal playground for children, and it is arguable that sea-bathing was the first important sport for women. Already in 1806 a visitor observed that people of inferior quality were coming to Scarborough – 'chiefly clothmakers and merchants from the West Riding; a set of honest, hearty fellows, who undermine the best constitutions in the world and die, by eating and drinking.'[24] An early reference to children at the seaside occurs in a guide-book to Scarborough in 1787: 'to observe the little animals fabricating their pies and castles in the sand,' wrote William Hutton in 1803, 'is a treat for a philosopher.'

The field sports continued to be the chief outdoor recreation of the aristocracy and gentry, and in the eighteenth century hunting gradually took its modern form. The encroachments of agriculture had confined stag-hunting to a few of the wilder areas such as Exmoor, and the place of hare-hunting was being taken by fox-hunting, which was more exciting and demanded more of the huntsman. Its full establishment took several generations. New skills had to be developed, faster strains of horse and hound were bred, the country was divided into regular hunts, and popular attitudes to the fox had to be changed: it had previously been freely destroyed as vermin. Harriers still outnumbered fox-hounds in 1835 but despite the laments of hare-hunting enthusiasts like Cobbett its supremacy was over, and – unless qualified – 'hunting' in Britain was henceforward more or less synonymous with hunting the fox.

All classes could enjoy the colour and excitement of a fox-hunt, and it did not directly threaten the larders of the poor. Shooting on the other hand led to growing tension. This was the inevitable result of intensified competition for limited numbers of game. It was made worse by the statutory restrictions and by the poverty of most country people. At first the shot-gun was almost as dangerous to the user as to the target, techniques were rudimentary, and exceptional skill was required to shoot birds on the wing; as guns became more accurate and destructive it became unsportsmanlike to shoot at sitting targets and to use methods such as netting and liming. The legal restrictions were severe. An Act of the Cavalier Parliament in 1671 forbade freeholders worth less than £100 a year to take game even on their own land, and the limit was higher for leaseholders. The bitterness caused by these restrictions was exacerbated by the acceleration of enclosure, the prevalence of rural poverty, and the spread of game preservation in the later eighteenth century. A 'poaching war' developed in which landowners stopped at little or nothing to protect their monopoly. This was justifiable by their own standards but as in other fields public indignation mounted at the savage penalties which were inflicted for trivial offences against property and the barbarous methods which were used to catch and deter poachers. The game laws were reformed by a long series of statutes beginning in 1827. Not only were they liberalised and humanised. In their revised form they proved to be at least as effective in protecting the rights of the sportsman.

There was to be no future for the grosser and more popular blood sports. Along with similar entertainments like public executions and the pillory they could not long survive what Joseph Strutt called in 1801 the 'general refinement of manners and prevalence of humanity among the moderns.' Bear and bull-baiting never in fact regained the popularity they enjoyed before the Civil War, and according to Strutt, by 1800 they existed only among 'the lowest and most despicable part of the people.' Cock-fighting, however, he described as still a 'fashionable divertissement.' Charles Cotton had said of it in *The Compleat Gamester* in 1674 that it was 'a sport or pastime so full of delight and pleasure, that I know not any game in that respect to be preferred to it.' In the eighteenth century cocking 'mains', which sometimes lasted several days, were attended by people of every rank, large sums were staked, and the chief events received national publicity. Cocking was similarly popular in Scotland, with the acquiescence of the clergy, no doubt because they had been brought up to it from their school-days.[25]

Attempts to ban bull-baiting – as much in the words of the Bill because of the 'idleness, rioting and drunkenness' it encouraged as for humanitarian reasons – narrowly failed in 1800 and 1802: Canning defended it in Parliament on the ground that it inspired courage and produced a nobleness of sentiment and elevation of mind. There was more in William Windham's criticism that the proposed restrictions were an infringement of liberty and involved discrimination against the amusements of the poor. Opinion was reacting fast against the callousness and brutality of the past but it was not until the 1830s and '40s that – largely owing to Richard ('Humanity') Martin – bull and bear-baiting and cock-fighting were at last abolished.

The decay of bear-baiting may have been connected with the rise of prize-fighting, which appealed to similar instincts and was also to be swept away in the humanitarian revolt. The 'gladiatorial' shows of the Restoration period from which eighteenth-century prize-fighting evolved were sometimes held in bear-gardens. As with modern all-in wrestling, there was an element of showmanship – the object was to gratify the spectators with the least possible damage to the fighters – but none the less they were sanguinary affairs in which swords, daggers and cudgels were used. By the middle of the eighteenth-century, popular tastes were becoming less bloodthirsty. Jack Broughton, champion of England from 1740 to 1750 and the leading promoter of his day, moved with the trend. A pugilist himself, he wanted to exclude other weapons than the fist, he framed the first rules for what later became boxing, he taught 'scientific' methods to his pupils, and he supplied them with primitive gloves for sparring. But prize-fighting continued to be dangerous and sometimes fatal even after fighting with the fists alone became normal later in the century.

Pugilism enjoyed its most resplendent phase in the Regency period. It was patronised by the nobility, vast sums were wagered, the big fights drew large crowds and aroused national interest. Along with others of doubtful character, it produced great champions such as Jem Belcher and Tom Cribb who owed their titles to outstanding skill and courage and were also honourable men. But in the changing climate of opinion it was doomed because of its brutality and of the crime and corruption which went with the large volume of gambling. After a few deaths in the 1820s and 1830s prize-fighting was driven underground by police action under the common law. It persisted in a dim half-world of secret rendezvous and special night trains until its final disappearance after the great fight – in the presence of Palmerston and for a stake of £250 – between Tom Sayers and the American champion, J. C. Heenan, in 1860.

The ancient sport of horse-racing gave rise to similar problems and met more complex needs. The race meeting was more than a sporting event and a medium for gambling. It was a social occasion for all classes and an opportunity for display on the part of owners, riders and spectators. Other popular amusements were provided. In the medieval tradition itinerant entertainers flocked to the courses. Until public gambling was forbidden there were booths for roulette and other games, and cocking mains were often held in connection with race meetings. Modern horse-racing owed much to royal patronage, which helped to make it fashionable, and more to science, which made it exciting. Charles II was a regular visitor to Newmarket, and William III started the custom of offering Royal Plates. More important was the evolution of the modern thoroughbred by careful breeding in a scientifically conscious age. Charles II imported six Arab and Barbary mares to improve the racing stock, and every thoroughbred racehorse in the world today is descended from three stallions imported by other owners between 1687 and 1729 – the Byerley Turk, the Darley Arabian and the Godolphin Arabian.[25]

Racing is still largely carried on within its eighteenth-century framework. It was then that Newmarket became the acknowledged national centre. Epsom, Ascot, Doncaster, Nottingham and Manchester were other important courses in the middle of the century, racing also flourished in Scotland, and many famous races were established: the St. Leger dates from 1776, the Oaks from 1779 and the Derby from 1780. The Jockey Club was formed as a dining club at Newmarket in about 1750 and began in the seventies to assume the national responsibility for regulating horse-racing. This was badly needed. Rules were non-existent, disregarded, or varied by agreement among the riders. Horses were untrained, jockeys unskilled, spectators out of control, corrupt practices widespread.

With the exception of cricket little need be said about the other sports. Yachting was introduced from Holland in the reign of Charles II, and billiards became popular – 'both a gentle cleanly and most ingenious game', said Charles Cotton. Village meetings at Whitsun and other holiday times kept alive the traditional sports. Wrestling, animal-baiting, dancing and pedestrianism were among the pastimes which were especially popular among the common people. Pedestrianism had a large following, and contests, sometimes for big wagers, attracted many spectators. Thames watermen competed for Doggett's Coat and Badge which was instituted in 1715; and there were the beginnings of modern rowing at the public schools. Bowls was still played widely under Charles II and was notorious for the crookedness which was associated with it. For reasons which are far from clear, it sank into obscurity in the eighteenth century. Strutt distinguished between bowling alleys, which had long been obsolete, and bowling greens, which had been popular within his memory but were less frequented than formerly. Archery enjoyed a short revival in the later eighteenth century: the Toxophilite Society was founded in 1781. Its popularity with women foreshadowed the era of croquet and lawn tennis. Golf was supreme in Scotland. 'They instruct their children in it, as soon as they can run alone', wrote an English visitor, Edward Topham, 'and grey hairs boast their execution.'[26] The rules were codified by the Company of Gentlemen Golfers at Edinburgh in 1744 and taken over by the club which was founded at St. Andrews in 1754 and became the 'Royal and Ancient' in 1834. Of football Strutt said that it had formerly been much in vogue among the common people, but 'of late years it seems to have fallen into disrepute, and is little practised'.

Cricket was the first modern team game. Little is known about its early history except that schoolboys at Guildford played a game called cricket in the middle of the sixteenth century. It was well developed by the time records become plentiful after 1700. Early recorded matches include London against Croydon in 1707, Kent against London in 1709, and the famous match between All England (drawn from Middlesex, Surrey and Sussex) and Kent in 1746. Kent won by a single run after two innings – the aggregate scores being 111 and 110. Like other games (including stool-ball,[27] from which it may have been derived), cricket was commonly played for money, and this may explain the lines on which it developed. Where large sums were at stake there was a heavy premium on skill, and representative matches were impossible without rules which were acceptable to both sides. It was no doubt because superior cricketing skills were scarce that teams included players of every class. Professionalism was taken for granted, and contemporaries marvelled, as posterity has done, that a nobleman would play under the captaincy of his gardener. In the search for improvement changes were made in equipment and techniques. Three stumps replaced two and straight bats curved ones. The Hambledon men were responsible for a new style in batting. Eleven became the normal (though by no means invariable) size of a team: it would be interesting to know by what process cricketers arrived at a decision which has had such far-reaching repercussions. The first general code of rules was compiled at the London Artillery Club in 1744, and the Marylebone Cricket Club, which was formed in 1788, gradually assumed the national responsibility for regulating the game. Cricketers everywhere readily deferred to the authority of the club which was particularly identified with the aristocracy. It was to the M.C.C. that it fell first to ban and then in 1835 to legalise the technical innovation – round-arm instead of under-arm bowling – which more perhaps than any other created modern cricket.

Though mainly localised in the South-East cricket was being played as far north as Yorkshire by the first half of the eighteenth century. It was well enough established by 1751 for the Sheffield authorities to engage professional cricketers 'to amuse the populace, and to draw them from cock-fighting exhibitions.'[28] By the same period it was beginning to be regarded as in a peculiar sense a national game. 'Hail cricket!' wrote James Love in a poem about the Kent and All England match of 1746, 'glorious, manly, British game! First of all sports! Be first alike in fame!' In the South-East village played against village, tradesmen against farmers, under 21s against over 21s, married men against bachelors, individuals against individuals in single wicket matches, and even females played. There were 10,000 spectators when three of Kent played three of England for £500 a side in London in 1743. In the public schools early intimations can be seen of the modern cult of sport. Cricket was being played at Eton and Westminster in the first half of the century, and Chester-field told his son at Westminster in 1745 that he should 'desire to excel all boys at cricket as well as in learning.' The headmaster of a High Wycombe preparatory school was explaining to parents in 1790 that 'the young gentlemen may qualify themselves for Eton in the manly game of cricket'[29], and the Marine Society were so impressed with its value for boys of other classes that they introduced it into the curriculum of their ship school at the same period.[30]

The addiction to gambling which was the common denominator among so many recreations should not be judged by later and especially Victorian standards. Attitudes had in general changed little since the Middle Ages, and few people looked upon moderate gambling as unethical. That cards should be played for money was taken for granted, and more or less everybody except Dissenters and Methodists bought chances in the State lotteries. Bets and wagers were laid on public events and every-day occurrences as well as on every kind of sport. The poor had their own gambling games such as pitch and toss and crown and anchor. Fashion in card games was fickle. Now ombre, now brag, now basset was popular and Horace Walpole admitted to an error in judgment in not learning 'wisk' or whist during its vogue in 1740s, because he thought it would be a passing rage. 'I wait in vain for its being left off,' he wrote in 1742. Commerce and hazard, which were better suited to high play, held their own among obsessive gamblers, and thousands were won and lost at them. Gambling was, as Charles Cotton had said, an 'enchanting witchery', 'gotten between idleness and avarice.' As always it bred parasites and attracted criminals. Countless crooks and sharpers exploited the greedy and the innocent at the clubs and watering-places, the race-courses, cock-pits and fair-grounds, and in the sale of forged tickets for the State lotteries.

Too little credit has perhaps been given to eighteenth-century Governments and Parliaments and to the law-enforcing agencies for the steps which were taken to deal with the worst abuses due to gambling. Private lotteries were banned in 1698, public gaming in 1744, and other legislation tried to keep pace with a never-ending succession of innovations and evasions. But the approach was pragmatic and not ideological. State lotteries, which had been held intermittently since 1566, and began to take place annually in 1776, did not come to an end until 1826. This was less because of moral qualms in the Treasury than that subscriptions had fallen off as responsible public opinion swung against the principle of State-supported gambling.

Drinking presented graver problems. The worst of them were due to spirit drinking. Distilling had been invented in Germany in the fifteenth century, but spirit drinking was not widespread in Britain until cheap spirits became readily available as a result of measures taken from 1690 onwards to foster the production of gin from home-grown corn. Not only were imports restricted but controls were removed from the manufacture and retailing of home-grown spirits. A side effect was to undermine the strict supervision which the magistrates often exercised over the alehouses. The steep increase in drinking was not confined to cheap gin. The consumption of wine grew rapidly after the Restoration, the Methuen Treaty of 1703 stimulated the drinking of port, and the production of malt for brewing reached record levels in the 1720s. In the same decade it was said that spirits were being sold at one house out of every seven in London: it was the era of 'Drunk for 1d. Dead drunk for 2d. Clean straw for nothing.' The toll in health and industrial efficiency was deadly. Several attempts were made to bring the situation under control despite riots and other popular protests and opposition from the vested interests, but it was not until the Acts of 1743 and 1751 that solutions were found which checked the worst evils.

Anxiety about popular uses of leisure – as symptoms of moral degeneracy – underlay the reform movements which occurred at the turn of the eighteenth and the nineteenth centuries. The first was premature, badly managed, and ineffectual. The second was timely, well managed, and successful.

The decline in religion and the notoriously evil living in high places after the Restoration were the more obvious of reasons for the first of these protests. In 1688 James II used the traditional method of a Royal Proclamation to call for the enforcement of the laws against vice and profanity, and with the support of the Crown and leaders of the Church numerous societies for the reformation of manners were formed in the nineties. The Almighty signified approval – at first somewhat unemphatically with a slight earthquake in 1692 but unequivocally in the great storm of 1703 when, said Defoe, every falling timber cried 'Repent.' Prostitution, gambling, drunkenness, obscene publications, plays, masquerades, and above all lax Sunday observance were attacked, and stricter enforcement of the law was demanded. Where this was not forthcoming the societies instituted proceedings themselves. At first they met with success, especially in the field of Sunday trading, but they alienated the Government and leading Churchmen by their criticisms of authority, and they lost popular support because of the methods they used to secure convictions and their apparent hypocrisy in attacking the pleasures of the poor but not the rich. 'These are all cobweb laws,' said Defoe, 'in which the small flies are caught, and the great ones break through.'

The first reform movement had exhausted itself by the 1730s, but protest was never silent. It came from many quarters including the Wesleys and the Fieldings and local authorities up and down the country, but it did not fully engage the establishment of Church and State again until the eighties and nineties.

More powerful forces were now at work. Beneath the second reform movement lay the hidden pressures of rapid industrialisation demanding new standards of industrial discipline. It was soon to be stimulated by fear of Jacobinism, and it had political and industrial backing which could not be ignored. Its leader, William Wilberforce, was close to the Prime Minister and exceptionally gifted in the political arts, and support came from law-enforcing agencies throughout the country. One of those who took the initiative was the Rev. Henry Zouch, a leading member of the West Riding bench, who was shocked by the breakdown in law and order which resulted from industrialisation. When the common people are drawn together upon any public occasion, he wrote in the middle eighties, 'a variety of mischiefs are certain to ensue; allured by unlawful pastimes, or even by vulgar amusements only, they wantonly waste their time and money to their own great loss and that of their employers.'[31]

Conditions were propitious for the issue at the instance of Wilberforce of a Royal Proclamation in 1787 calling for the enforcement of the laws against immorality, excessive drinking, and the violation of the Sabbath. It was accompanied by letters to Lords Lieutenant from the Secretary of State, it was to be read in churches four times a year, and was followed by the establishment of the Proclamation Society, which was organised by a group led by Wilberforce to mobilise support for the policy.

The Proclamation Society, the Society for the Suppression of Vice and the Encouragement of Religion and Virtue which was set up in 1802 and soon superseded it, and innumerable other societies with similar objects campaigned for the same causes as the societies for the reformation of manners a century earlier and as the Puritans before them. They laid special stress on the enforcement of the law relating to Sunday observance. This was inevitable, and it was also well advised. Not only was Sabbatarianism a matter of deep conviction among both Evangelical and other supporters of the movement. Working-class misuse of the Sabbath offended against the conventional upper-class view of the way Sunday should be kept – at least by others: George III agreed with the Proclamation but refused to set an example by discontinuing the Sunday band concerts at Windsor. All knew of the drunkenness and disorder which occurred on Sundays and of the absenteeism which followed on Mondays and Tuesdays.

It was only a short step to the denial of popular recreations at other times. Christmas, Easter and Whitsuntide, the only seasons of festival in England, said Robert Southey, were 'always devoted by artificers and the peasantry to riot and intoxication'. His remedy was to provide more holidays. It was the want of holidays, he thought, which 'breaks down and brutalises the labouring class', and where they occurred seldom they were uniformly abused. With growing confidence the societies on the other hand went on to attack almost every form of recreation from gambling, horse-racing and bull-baiting and obscene publications to fairs, theatres, concerts and rural sports. Encouraged by success they also moved increasingly towards the extreme Sabbatarianism of which Daniel Webster was to be the chief exponent. 'Amusement, recreation, pastimes, indolent repose, satisfactions in worldly company, worldly society, worldly banquets', all, wrote Webster in *The Lord's Day* (1831), must cease on the Sabbath, and exercises of religion must fill the day. Wyclif could have asked for no more.

The other side did not go unstated. An eccentric and endearing minority of people in authority shared the views of Sir Thomas Beevor who dissented in 1787 from proposals before the Norfolk Quarter Sessions to give effect to the Proclamation. He refused to agree that the poor were more vicious or abandoned than their forefathers. To limit the number of alehouses would be oppressive, because it would 'tend to deprive the poor of a great part of that scanty pittance of happiness which their lot in this life can afford.'[32] As already noted, a strong body of conservative opinion sympathised with William Windham when he opposed the proposal to abolish bull-baiting in 1802 because it was no crueller than hunting and the Bill was part of a system to deprive the lower classes of all their amusements. Critics of

Wilberforce charged him with ignoring the vices of the rich and powerful. This was fair comment. It is impossible to say whether it was due to lack of courage, self-deception or a realistic appreciation of the best long-term strategy for achieving his objectives. Judged by the results it was a wise move. Opposition was reduced, and – measured in the perspective of history – upper-class debauchees and Sabbath-breakers had only a short respite. All were to be caught up in the second and greater triumph of puritanism to which the reform movement was a prelude.

4

AFTER THE INDUSTRIAL REVOLUTION

By the 1830s the medieval system of holidays was in the final stages of dissolution. Christmas, Easter and Whitsun were still generally regarded as holiday seasons, and in some areas a few of the other traditional holidays were still kept, but in much of industry Christmas was the only recognised holiday apart from Sundays. Christmas Day and Good Friday were the only full holidays which the Factory Act of 1833 prescribed for children under 12 in the textile mills, and some manufacturers took advantage of a loophole under which if the children consented they could be employed even then.

The same trends affected office workers. The Bank of England closed on 47 holidays in 1761, 40 in 1825, 18 in 1830, and four in 1834 – Good Friday, Christmas Day, May Day and 1 November. In 1797 the Customs offices closed on seven of the Twelve Days of Christmas, by 1840 only on Christmas Day. Lamenting in 1818 that as a clerk at India House he had only one day off at Christmas, Charles Lamb looked back to the 'pretty garnish of St. John's Day, Holy Innocents etc.' that used to 'bestud it all round in the calendar.'

This was not all. The old holidays were losing what little remained of their former character. Of Christmas Day itself Leigh Hunt wrote in 1823 that it was scarcely worth mention in London, and an American visitor in 1843 that there was nothing to it except dinner parties.[33] As for Sunday, the remaining opportunities for amusements other than drinking were being further circumscribed by Sabbatarian pressure and urban development. As the Secretary of the Handloom Weavers Commission said of Manchester operatives in 1840, many working people spent Sunday either in drinking or in inactive idleness. It was no wonder that a startling increase in drunkenness followed the virtual removal of controls on the sale of beer in 1830 – what the Webbs called the leading case of legislation based on abstract theory. And as building encroached on the available land there were often not even the open spaces 'calculated for public walks' which the Select Committee on the Health of Towns (1840) thought 'essential to the health and comfort of the poorer classes', though the first public park was established at Derby in that year on private initiative (*cf.* Seaborne, *Education*, pl. 142).

To some – the stricter Sabbatarians, the doctrinaires who refused to recognise Christmas Day because it was pagan and popish, those who saw moral danger in all popular amusements – the denial of recreations was desirable in itself. Others looked upon it as the permanent lot of most of mankind. After all, as the Home Secretary, Sir James Graham, told Parliament in 1847, 'throughout this world of sorrow and of care, the lot of eating, drinking, working and dying, must ever be the sum of human life among the masses of a large portion of the human family.'[34]

It was in fact an unstable situation. The vacuum could not long remain unfilled. As the national income grew, improved hours and holidays could not be withheld indefinitely from working people. Particularly in the period of increasing prosperity after 1850 there was mounting pressure for better conditions, and employers slowly came to realise that better provision for rest and recreation was essential to industrial efficiency and less objectionable than absenteeism. By the end of the century attitudes towards leisure had been revolutionised, and a new pattern of holidays had emerged in response to the needs of a largely industrialised society with a modern system of communications: by the 1880s about two-thirds of the population of England and Wales lived in towns.

No doubt the curtailment of holidays and the stricter enforcement of Sunday observance were an indispensable stage in the process of industrialisation and in the introduction of methods of industrial discipline suited to the new requirements. They came about through the operation of impersonal forces of which the Evangelical movement was one expression. What was gradually to take the place of the old system similarly owed little to conscious planning. It was the result of piecemeal developments in which scarcely any of the initiative came from Government and Parliament. For the most part it was the cumulative product of empirical decisions by individual employers, pressures from trade unions, changing attitudes to work and leisure as prosperity grew, and the efforts of humanitarians primarily concerned with the welfare of women and children in industry. One of the few attempts to look at the problem as a whole was made by the House of Lords when it discussed the Bank Holidays Bill promoted by Sir John Lubbock in 1871.

The most important innovation was the weekly half-holiday. By the fifties the building trades in some towns were stopping work at 4 o'clock on Saturdays but the Saturday half-holiday did not begin to become common until the spread of the sixty-hour week in the sixties and seventies. It was the more highly valued because of the denial of Sunday amusements and many people were glad to work longer on other days in order to secure it. By 1878 the term 'weekend' was in use for a peculiarly British institution which some foreigners envied and others saw as evidence of national decadence. The weekly half-holiday was still not universal in 1914 but the extent to which it was regarded as normal was shown by the passage of the Shops Act of 1912 which had the effect in practice of guaranteeing it to shop assistants. This followed prolonged agitation in which Lubbock (by now Lord Avebury) took a leading part.

In 1871 Christmas Day and Good Friday were the only bank holidays apart from Sundays. Lubbock's Act added Boxing Day, Easter Monday and Whit Monday, which were already widely kept as holidays, and created an entirely new holiday on the first Monday in August. Yet as recently as 1868 he had withdrawn an earlier Bill because Parliament had refused to include Boxing Day in view of the inconvenience to business. It was indicative of the speed with which opinion was changing that despite the refusal of Government backing Lubbock felt able in 1871 to include not only Boxing Day but an additional summer bank holiday. He proposed a new and frankly secular holiday divorced from the religious festivals and on a date chosen to meet the needs of the beneficiaries. For tactical reasons he limited the Bill to bank clerks but he always expected that the new bank holidays would become general. Observance of the first Whitsun and August bank holidays was only partial but in 1872 *The Times* commented that August Bank Holiday was all but universally observed and had acquired 'at least as decisive acceptance as the old traditional Holydays.'

The other major innovation was the 'summer holiday' – the recognised annual absence from work usually of a week or a fortnight which by 1914 was taken for granted by most professional people and was spreading among wage-earners. Already by the sixties and seventies a holiday of up to a fortnight with pay was common in offices. Dons, school teachers, barristers and civil servants had clung to treatment which was much more generous. Examples of paid holidays for manual workers – perhaps two or three days in the year – are recorded in the seventies[35]. By the nineties they were common in public utilities and local authorities – even in exceptional cases to the extent of two weeks. But pay or no pay, more and more manual workers were taking holidays away from home. Lancashire cotton towns had their wakes weeks, factories closed for works holidays, hundreds of thousands went on day excursions to the rapidly growing holiday resorts.

Two concepts with far-reaching implications were gaining acceptance. Holidays were beginning to be regarded as a positive good which should be open to all, and reasonable holidays as a right to which workers were entitled from employers. Leisure and rest, when turned to good account, said Alfred Marshall in the *Principles of Economics* (1890), were necessary for the efficiency of the labour force.[36] Some peers thought that Lubbock's Bill did not go far enough. Lord Overstone suggested that the new holidays should be called general holidays and that the opportunities of relaxation they provided should be open to everybody in this hard-working country. Lord Redesdale wanted to add the first Mondays in February and November. Six holidays a year would not be too much, he said, for persons closely confined to business and they should be equally distributed over the year. To go without a holiday because of poverty was beginning to be looked upon as a mark of deprivation. In the seventies and eighties the provision of holidays for groups such as poor clergy, invalid children and slum families became an accepted charitable object which was pursued by many philanthropic agencies.

In this dynamic situation Sunday was almost but not entirely a fixed point. Opinion was by no means united but reformers such as the founders of the National Sunday League in 1855 who believed that the Sabbath would be strengthened if improving recreations were permitted made slow headway against fanatical and well-organised opposition. In 1852 the Churches forced Derby to rescind a decision to allow Sunday opening of the Crystal Palace: it was pointed out that nations such as France and Italy which profaned the Sabbath had suffered bloodshed and revolution. More or less everybody shuddered at the prospect of introducing the dreaded 'Continental Sunday', though most people acquiesced in Sunday postal deliveries and the Sunday trading which was widespread. It took forty years of agitation before Parliament agreed in 1896 to the Sunday opening of State museums and art galleries: Manchester had pointed the way in 1877.

The Victorian Sabbath was highly resistant to frontal attack but it was to be undermined by more insidious influences as church attendances fell off, and even many churchgoers began to doubt whether it was wrong to indulge in innocent pleasures which were permissible on week-days and involved nobody else in additional Sunday labour. The Lord's Day Observance Society (which had been founded in 1831) might be able to stop public authorities from providing Sunday concerts and opening recreation grounds. It could restrain but not in the last resort stop the desecration of the Sabbath on the croquet lawns and tennis courts of suburbia or by thousands of young people who – on bicycles made for one or two – transported themselves to the country on summer Sundays after the invention of the safety bicycle and the pneumatic tyre in the eighties. And close behind the bicycle came the motor car with a thirst for petrol and a susceptibility to breakdown which made no distinction between week-day and Sabbath.

Christmas underwent an astonishing transformation. Little had been left of the 'old Christmas' except vague associations of good will and a tradition of feasting and merriment. Within fifty years it was reshaped in its present form. Except for evergreen decorations and the Christmas dinner all the main customs of the modern Christmas date from the Victorian period: and none of them was due either to the Prince Consort or to Charles Dickens. The Christmas tree, which was of Alsatian origin, began to take root in England in the thirties and was fully naturalised by the fifties. The Christmas card was an English invention which met the need for a convenient method of exchanging good wishes with distant relatives and friends. It died out after a false start in the forties, but established itself quickly after it was discovered afresh in the sixties. The carol had practically disappeared: people spoke of 'the Christmas carol' in the singular because they only knew one – 'God rest ye merry, gentlemen.' Its successful revival in the seventies and eighties was an offshoot of the revival of hymn-singing. Santa Claus was an American immigrant of Dutch descent who made a scarcely-noticed first appearance in England in the seventies but by the nineties had ousted (and often usurped the name of) the traditional Father Christmas – a grey-bearded personification of the season who had never been identified with children or had any previous associations with chimneys and stockings.[37] The giving of presents was a late Victorian revival of the obsolescent custom of New Year gifts.

Shorter working hours, longer holidays, better communications, more to spend. How were the new opportunities for leisure used? For the most part things went on as before. The additional leisure and the means to enjoy it were unevenly distributed. The chief beneficiaries were the better-paid salaried workers and the skilled craftsmen who were the aristocracy of labour. The old, the sick, the unemployed, families with young children, mostly lived at or below the bare subsistence level. In parts of East London at the end of the century half the population were either in chronic want or under a constant struggle to obtain the necessities of life. Conditions in rural areas were almost as bad as in the poorer districts of the cities. Older people were slow to change their ways, and the women were tied by prejudice – shared by themselves – to a restricted range of activities centred on home and church or chapel. The prevailing ethic in any case allowed little room for pleasure as it had usually been understood throughout history.

Except among the stricter sects life was not, however, as gloomy as is often supposed. The conventional restraints bore lightly on some of the very rich and most of the very poor, and a vigorous popular culture adapted to urban conditions developed among the lower middle and upper working classes. Popular musical taste found such outlets as the brass band movement of the North, choral singing in the Welsh valleys, hymn-singing everywhere: the piano in the parlour symbolised affluence and a proper musical appreciation. It was the heyday of the pantomime and the music-hall. Musical evenings and whist drives, hurdy gurdies and freak shows, billiard halls and working men's clubs, wax works, panoramas, reading circles, sewing bees, circuses, picnics and Christy minstrels – all would have a place in a comprehensive picture of Victorian recreations. There was also a seamier side exemplified by the betting dens, the traffic in obscene publications, the rat-killing matches and the brothels which flourished in the great cities.

We shall concentrate on the three major developments which chiefly anticipated the future. The Victorian age for all practical purposes saw the beginnings of modern tourism, the mass media of entertainment, and modern sport.

The railway was the great liberator which set the people free to travel. 'I rejoice to see it,' wrote Thomas Arnold, 'and think that feudality is gone for ever.' Of the thousands leaving Manchester by excursion train at Whitsuntide in 1845 the *Manchester Guardian* wrote: 'The birth of this new and cheap means of transit is as if the wings of the wind have been given for a week to the closely confined operative, the hard-working mechanic, and the counter-riveted shopkeeper. They enjoy the needful relaxation from the toil or care or confinement of business; they see new scenes and acquire new tastes for the beautiful in nature as, whirled along by the steam-car, they rush 'forth to fresh fields, and pastures new'.' It was in the same year that a young artisan and temperance worker, Thomas Cook, decided to devote himself whole-time to organising the railway excursions which were to make him famous.

In the wake of the upper classes, the new holidaymakers flowed mainly to the coast, and large seaside resorts grew up within access of all the main centres of population. By 1900 three of the seven largest resorts were serving the industrial North. Blackpool, which had become the chief holiday playground of Lancashire and Yorkshire operatives, grew from 6,000 inhabitants in 1871 to 47,000 in 1901. Beneath subtle differences in social status there were great similarities between the many resorts. Life was focussed on the simple pleasures of beach and promenade and pier, the social unit was the family, and typical institutions were the bathing machine and the deck chair, the donkey ride and the pierrot.

The railway also opened up the cities and holiday resorts of the Continent to increasing numbers of British tourists. Some went abroad to avoid the plebeian crowds on the English beaches or to escape to German gaming rooms and the forbidden pleasures of Paris. Most followed the well-trodden tourist routes in search of culture and natural beauty. Thomas Cook entered the international business in 1855, and by the seventies Cook's tourists – mainly drawn from the middle classes – were as well known abroad as the English 'milords' had been. Others pioneered new forms of holiday-making unobtainable at home. Alpine mountaineering made a special appeal to intellectuals. 'We live for the most part in a very iron mask of forms,' wrote Frederic Harrison, who was a leading member of the Alpine Club which was formed in 1857, 'we must be free and simple sometimes, or we break.' Steamships were being used as early as the 1830s for holiday cruises to destinations such as Greece and the Holy Land: by the nineties there were cruises to Norway for eight guineas. The Cyclists' Touring Club arranged its first Continental tour in 1879 and published its first *Continental Road Book* in 1887. And it was largely due to Henry Lunn and other young Englishmen that after the introduction of skiing from Norway Switzerland began in the last quarter of the century to develop into a winter as well as a summer playground.

New forms of transport extended the opportunities for travel. The bicycle was cheaper and more flexible than the railway, and even before the cycling boom of the nineties, when the cyclist still shared the country roads with hen and horse, the pioneers began the rediscovery of the countryside which prepared the way for the motoring age. In 1896 the motorist was freed from the requirement that a man with a red flag must precede him and from speed limits of 2 m.p.h. in the towns and

4 m.p.h. outside them. In 1903 the speed limit was raised to 20 m.p.h. and it stayed
there until 1930. Private motoring was at first a hobby of the wealthy, and the
number of private cars was only 132,000 in 1914. But Henry Ford's Model T was
already in mass production at Detroit, and William Morris, later Lord Nuffield, had
turned his main attention from bicycles to motor cars.

By the mass media of entertainment we do not mean simply forms of entertainment
for the masses. In this sense the medieval minstrels, the Tudor theatres and bear-
gardens, and the eighteenth century prize-fighters were mass entertainers. What was
new in the nineteenth and twentieth centuries was not so much that there were vastly
greater audiences as the use of new techniques to reach them without a personal
relationship between entertainer and entertained. This had of course been true of
printing, and reading (or being read to) had been a recreation long before Caxton.
It was not, however, until the seventeenth and eighteenth centuries that the market
for recreational reading was systematically exploited on a large scale nor until the
nineteenth on a mass one.

The turning-point came with the newspaper, the magazine, the novel and the
circulating library: the first circulating library seems to have been opened at Edinburgh in 1725. Each to a greater or less extent sought to entertain the reader as well
as to inform or edify him. Much prejudice – an aspect of the Puritan tradition – had
to be overcome before light reading became generally acceptable. 'A circulating
library,' said Sir Anthony Absolute, was 'an ever-green tree of diabolical knowledge.' According to Coleridge in 1817, light reading was 'a sort of beggarly day-
dreaming' aimed at reconciling 'the two contrary yet coexisting propensities of
human nature, namely, indulgence of sloth, and hatred of vacancy.' It could also be
positively harmful. The passions and crimes and follies with which writers of fiction
fed their readers were a source of moral danger especially to the young, the uneducated
and the female sex. Others were afraid that for this reason literacy would further
demoralise the working classes. To Benthamites reading for pleasure was a
frivolous use of time better spent in the acquisition of useful knowledge.

The trend towards mass literacy was irresistible. It was essential to economic and
social efficiency, it was necessary for the promotion of good causes such as temperance
and Bible-reading, and it was dictated by the extension of the franchise. Before
Forster's Education Act of 1870 the majority of working people had decided the
matter for themselves, and Scotland was ahead of England and Wales. Meanwhile
technological and other changes stimulated reading. With the spread of gas-lighting
in the towns and paraffin lamps in the country it began to be pleasurable to read in
the winter evenings; and the widening use of spectacles opened the eyes of many
thousands to the printed word. A number of inventions and marketing innovations
in the middle of the century brought down the cost of books and periodicals, and
after the repeal of the paper duties in 1861 newspapers and magazines at last ceased
to be free of any taxation.

The new demands were met at various levels. Sales which were sensational by
earlier standards were achieved by the still highly priced magazines and novels which
catered for the better-educated public. *Uncle Tom's Cabin*, which had a wider appeal,
sold 150,000 copies within six months of publication in England in 1852. Serialisation
vastly extended the market for Dickens and other popular novelists. *Punch* (1841)
and the *Illustrated London News* (1842) broke new ground in magazine production.

The Public Libraries Act became law by a narrow majority in 1850 after being hotly opposed on political and social grounds. The brewers joined in because its supporters claimed that it would reduce the volume of drinking: advocates of public libraries drew attention to the shameful contrast with the much better provision in Western Europe and the United States. The first national commercial libraries were established. The pioneer, Charles Edward Mudie, who had started his famous library in 1842, accepted a responsibility for ensuring that his shelves would contain nothing which was morally contaminating. W. H. Smith's chain was started in 1852, but Boot's – which was aimed at a wider public – not until 1900.

The mass reading public consisted mainly of the lower middle classes, the skilled artisans and the higher-grade domestic servants. Comparatively few of them turned to the public libraries and fewer still could afford to patronise Mr. Mudie. They included many readers of serious fiction – above all Dickens – but the vast majority could not rise so high. Millions of copies were, however, sold of 'family' papers like the *Family Herald*, the cheaper religious weeklies, and respectable Sunday newspapers, like the *News of the World*. In so far as the 'lower classes' read at all they found their literary recreation in the less reputable Sunday papers which specialised in scandal and crime and the broadsheets no more edifying in character which sold in millions for a halfpenny or a penny. At their best these contained highly sentimentalised serials with titles such as *Fatherless Fanny, or the Mysterious Orphan*. Often – in a long tradition of popular entertainment by no means confined to the less educated – they consisted of sordid accounts of actual or imaginary crimes and sensational stories on horrific themes like the exploits of Sweeney Todd the demon barber, the activities of vampires and werewolves, the hidden secrets of infamous convents.

Some saw grounds for optimism in the spread of reading in any form. After all, as Wilkie Collins said in 1858, 'the Unknown Public' had scarcely begun to read in a literary sense. Credit should, he thought, be given to the penny journals for discovering a new public, and in an age devoted to the inevitability of progress, it would only be a matter of time before it commanded the services of the best writers. Increasing literacy would not, however, in itself have provided a solution. There was too wide a gap between the penny journals, the popular Sunday newspapers and even the 'family' papers on the one hand and on the other the newspapers, magazines and novels which were read by the educated.

Chief among those who exploited the opportunities for profit by filling this gap were the three men, George Newnes, Alfred Harmsworth and Arthur Pearson, who were the main pioneers of the modern style of mass journalism in Britain. They discovered – indeed in large measure created – the vast market which was latent among the more intelligent products of the elementary schools – eager to read yet unsatisfied by what had hitherto been available and handicapped by an education which had in most cases ended before their teens. 'I am the average man,' Newnes said of himself later, and the formula which proved so successful was epitomised in the name *Tit-bits* which he gave to the new magazine which he launched in 1881. Essentially it consisted of the anecdotal presentation of news and facts along with lighter matter such as jokes and riddles with a view to entertainment as well as information and with scrupulous regard to the proprieties. Harmsworth's *Answers* (1885) and *Pearson's Weekly* (1890) shared in the spectacular success of *Tit-bits*.

It was the beginning of a new era in magazine and newspaper journalism. 'Mincemeat which requires no chewing,' said Edward Dowden in 1889. The *Strand*, which Newnes started in 1891, was the most famous of the new-style magazines which were launched in the nineties: published on Saturday for Sunday reading and intended for a better-educated public than *Tit-bits*, it quickly reached a circulation of nearly half a million. The breakthrough into daily journalism came with the establishment of the *Daily Mail* by Harmsworth in 1896. It cost a halfpenny, and for the first time substantial numbers of working people began to read a daily paper. Harmsworth's imaginative attempt to develop a popular daily for women in the *Daily Mirror* (1903) proved, however, to be premature.

Of the other mass media only the cinema made much headway before 1914. Though Edison's phonograph had been patented in 1877 the gramophone was still not much more than a toy. Wireless telegraphy was only used for military and business purposes. The moving picture was a natural sequel to still photography and to popular forms of visual entertainment like the panorama and the magic lantern show. The first public film show was held in Paris in 1895, the first in London in 1896. The main places of exhibition at first were music-halls, fair-grounds and shops, and it was some time before film-making broke away from the music-hall and fair-ground traditions. *The Great Train Robbery* in 1903 foreshadowed the modern feature film. The transition was symbolised by the first appearance on the screen in 1914 of Charles Chaplin, the English music-hall artist who was to be the greatest figure in film history. By 1907 the first theatre wholly devoted to films had been opened – the Balham Empire. The middle classes looked down on the 'pictures' with slowly diminishing disapproval and blamed them for truancy and juvenile crime. By 1914 there were some 4,000 cinemas in Great Britain, and the 'pictures' had taken firm hold among the working classes, especially women and children. In 1912 Philip Snowden included the 'pictures' with the music-hall, cheap periodicals and books among the new items of expenditure which were necessities for the working classes.[38]

No changes in the use of leisure were to have more far-reaching repercussions than those in sport. The seeds went further back. Most of the raw material was provided by traditional games and by the traditional love of sport, and what happened in the middle of the nineteenth century had been anticipated in the eighteenth by the story of cricket and the beginnings of modern sport in the public schools. There had been other foretastes like the first amateur sculling championship in 1830 and the formation of the first figure skating club in the same year. Despite the support of Bentham and Brougham gymnastics and physical training, which became popular on the Continent under the influence of Rousseau's educational ideas, did not, however, establish themselves to the same extent in Britain.

Roughly within a generation the old ingredients were transmuted into something which was largely new. The explanations which are commonly given are inadequate. The cult of sport did not originate in the pedagogical theories of Dr. Arnold and other progressive headmasters nor in a conscious or unconscious attempt to train young men for the responsibilities of emergent Empire. It seems to have arisen from the spontaneous reactions of many people to the needs of an industrialised and urbanised society with a puritanical and competitive ethic. Sport provided channels for the energies of youth – whether confined within boarding schools or city streets – which were less degrading and less damaging to society than hooliganism, gambling, drink and indiscriminate sex. It not only provided controlled outlets for violence and other anti-social tendencies.* It was positively beneficial to health and working efficiency. It imposed its own discipline, and team games were a training in loyalty and coopera- tion. Nor were the benefits confined to youth. Adults were looking for new pastimes in keeping with the ethos of the age which they could pursue under urban conditions. Croquet and lawn tennis developed more or less in parallel with modern football. Spectators at a demonstration of football at a Liverpool cricket ground in 1857 were asked to judge 'if this new sport was a worthy manner for gentlemen to employ themselves with on a Saturday afternoon as a change from the common one of rabbit coursing.'[39] And sport proved to have the further advantage of providing enter- tainment – and an emotional outlet – for large numbers of people, especially working men on their Saturday afternoons, who did not play games but participated vicar- iously as spectators or newspaper readers.

The pedagogy, the philosophy and the theology at most added impetus to a movement which was already under way. As far as the public schools were concerned the new outlook on sport seems to have evolved from an unconscious recognition of the inadequacies of the traditional boarding-school regime among the boys them- selves. With a few noteworthy exceptions such as Christopher Wordsworth at Win- chester, most schoolmasters before the fifties were out of sympathy with the im- portance the boys attached to sporting prowess, were indifferent or hostile to the games the boys organised among themselves, and positively disapproved of com- petitive matches with other schools. At the universities sport took a subordinate place until at least the fifties, and, with the exception of the field sports, had little or none in the lives of most adults even of the upper classes. Nor at first did it dominate school life. In their free time the boys continued to hunt and fish, drink and gamble, even collect butterflies and botanical specimens. Arnold's own approach was practical rather than ideological. His own preference was probably for individualistic activities like swimming and gymnastics, but, despite the violence with which football was played at Rugby, he thought that it was a better outlet for the animal spirits of school- boys than mutinies and public rowdyism. Other headmasters began to encourage organised games for similar reasons: it was part of Cotton's policy for restoring Marl- borough after the disastrous mutinies of the early fifties. Arnold's main contribution was indirect. There is little doubt that the spread of organised games in the public schools – and certainly the introduction of compulsory games – was an offshoot of the self-government by the boys which he pioneered.

Belief in sport as an aid to character-building which was essential to a Christian education came next. It was an aspect of the Victorian enthusiasm for 'manliness'. Whereas Coleridge and Arnold had identified it with maturity, Charles Kingsley, Thomas Hughes and other 'muscular Christians' emphasised the masculine qualities of courage and physical vitality. This made a natural appeal to most boys. It was popularised by Hughes' *Tom Brown's Schooldays*, which was published in 1857, but by then, as Fitzjames Stephen said in a review of the book, games had already become 'exercises and tasks, the performance of which is enforced by far stronger sanctions than any which the authorities of the school have it in their power to apply.' It in-

* Writing of his enthusiasm for football, a young apprentice of the 1960s summed it up very well. 'In football you can let out any pent up energy inside you without doing any real serious damage. What I mean by serious damage is breaking windows, chairs and other articles of furniture etc. . . . A great game.' (Ethel Venables, *The Young Worker at College* [1967], 76)

fluenced Bradley, Temple, Thring and other leading headmasters of the sixties and seventies: the playing of games, said Thring, contributed to the 'manliness' which had made the English such an adventurous race. The Clarendon Commission on the Public Schools in 1864 paid tribute to the part of cricket and football in character-training. It was in a missionary spirit that sportsmen from the public schools carried the message to the boys' clubs and school missions which were set up to convert and civilise the youth of the slums. It was one of the civilising tools which public-schoolmen took with them to the backward parts of the world as clergymen and administrators – and for that matter to the grammar schools at which they taught at home. Everywhere church activity was closely related to the new enthusiasm for sport. Aston Villa, Bolton Wanderers, Queens Park Rangers and Everton are among the famous football clubs which were offshoots of churches.

By the eighties and nineties a comprehensive range of sports had developed. Between them they catered for both sexes, most ages and most tastes. Most of them were either new or so much changed from their prototypes as to be substantially new. Governing bodies had been set up, rules standardised and humanized, new techniques evolved and national and even international competitions organised. They were dissociated from gambling and typically they were played for their own sake: most were 'amateur' and where there were professionals their status was inferior. With Association football as the most important exception they were largely identified with the upper and upper middle classes, and the pattern which was established during the seminal period has been substantially unaltered since, even down to the social nuances by which the various sports were differentiated. By later standards the numbers who engaged in sport were still tiny: even in soccer there were only about 1,000 clubs in England and Wales in 1888 and about 8,000 in 1900. But a movement was set in train which has not yet gone into reverse. Fair play, sportsmanship, amateurism, and the sovereignty of the referee are among the hitherto unfamiliar concepts which developed concurrently and spread more or less intact from Britain to the world.

Cricket was least affected by the revolution. Yet even so the greatest days of cricket did not begin until the sixties. It had not spread fast earlier in the century, and abuses such as the fixing of matches, which would no longer be regarded as cricket, had only gradually been eradicated. Overarm bowling was legalised in 1864, and in 1862 a schoolboy of 14, W. G. Grace, began a career in which he was to dominate cricket for a generation. Grace typified the talented public-schoolmen who provided the leadership in sport during the formative years but he was only one of a number of great amateurs whose skill and personalities popularised cricket as a game to play and to watch. In 1870 there were 22 county matches. In 1873 nine counties began what became the County Championship. By the end of the century there were fifteen first-class counties, and only two – Northampton in 1905 and Glamorgan in 1921 – were added later. The first matches between England and Australia were held in 1877, and the Ashes were invented in 1882.

Modern football had to be created almost anew. It evolved not from the village games but from the no less bloody and disorganised versions which had developed in leading public schools. Each had its peculiarities – still to be seen at Eton and Winchester – and competitive football outside closed communities was impossible until at any rate basically common rules were agreed. By the middle of the century, when the game was still played almost exclusively by present and former public-school boys, two main versions had emerged, a dribbling and a handling one, but there were still many variants and supporters of both aimed at a common code. The Football Association, which was founded in 1863, was intended to be the sole national authority, but a minority of London clubs refused to accept a majority decision against the abolition of hacking (intentionally kicking an opponent's shins) and formed the Rugby Football Union in 1871. Any remaining prospects of reconciliation were killed by sharp disagreements over professionalism which became acute in the eighties.

What was superficially in dispute was a question of ideology which could not have arisen at any earlier period or so readily at any later one. Was the payment of players – which was taken for granted in cricket – compatible with the amateur principle of playing games for their own sake? Underlying this was the question whether working-class players should be excluded from first-class football. Should it continue to be dominated by the middle-class pioneers? It came to a head because of the speed with which working men took to the game as players and spectators. It was not simply that wage-earners could not afford to lose pay in order to play in away matches. Provision for spectators involved expenditure which had to be recouped by charging for admission. The crowds identified themselves with the home team, gates varied according to its success, and it was important to attract the best players. Large sums were soon at stake. When Aston Villa first charged for admission in 1874 the takings were 5s.3d: in 1904 over £14,000 was taken at a single match. Leading clubs competed for the top players, and even before the Football Association legalised professionalism in 1885, the Northern and Midland clubs, which relied on working-class players who were professionals in all but name, had established their ascendancy over the Southern clubs whose teams were mainly public-school men. After Old Etonians were beaten by Blackburn Olympic in the Cup Final of 1883 the Cup did not return to the South until it was regained by Tottenham Hotspur in 1901. The F.A. Cup had been instituted in 1871 : C. W. Alcock, the Secretary of the Association, is said to have derived the idea from knockout tournaments he had known as a boy at Harrow. The league system, which was based on American precedents, came later. The Football League was formed in 1888 and quickly became the model for competitive soccer at all levels. Probably nothing did more to popularise the game with both players and spectators.

The Rugby Union stood out against professionalism. They did not accept the logic of Alcock, who was Secretary of the Surrey County Cricket Club as well as of the F.A. 'I can't see,' he said at one of the critical discussions about professionalism in 1885, 'why men should not labour at football as at cricket.' The price was a lasting split on class and territorial lines when the Northern clubs broke away from the Union in 1895 over the issue of professionalism and developed their own distinctive form of Rugby football. It also perpetuated a cleavage between soccer and rugger based on social distinctions, and assured the future of soccer as the chief winter sport. Cup Final attendances rose from 4,000 in 1880 to 45,000 in 1893 and 110,000 in 1901. Middle-class critics were alarmed by the mass hysteria of the crowds at League and Cup matches – at the bad sportsmanship, the baiting of referees, the alternation between rage and jubilation. More sympathetic observers noted the pride and loyalty and identification with the community which the games brought out.

Golf, as Arthur James Balfour said, was well suited to busy men, and it was adapted to most ages and levels of skill especially after the introduction of the rubber core ball in 1902. Yet in contrast with Scotland it began and continued as a largely middle-class game in England. The first club for English players as distinct from Scottish exiles was Westward Ho!, which was founded in 1864, but the game did not make much headway until the eighties. The British Open Championship which was started in 1860 was played on Scottish courses until the nineties but the first amateur championship in 1885 was organised by the Royal Liverpool at Hoylake. The St. Andrews Ladies Club began in 1867; the Ladies Golf Union was formed in 1893.

The need for a game suitable for both sexes to play together was only partly met by archery and golf and by two innovations of the fifties and sixties, croquet and badminton. Croquet, which was probably imported from Ireland in the early fifties, quickly became popular as a country-house and suburban game, and an All England Croquet Club was formed at semi-rural Wimbledon in 1868. Badminton, a derivative of battledore and shuttlecock, which is thought to have been invented at a country-house party, made little progress in England until it was reintroduced from India where the firstcode was framed in 1877.

There remained a gap. It was filled by lawn tennis, which was the result of deliberate attempts to adapt real tennis to the open air. Major Walter Wingfield, who patented his 'New and Improved Court for Playing the Ancient Game of Tennis' in 1874, was one of several people who had been experimenting on these lines, and he exploited the idea skilfully in a market which was eager to be discovered. Wisely abandoning the original name 'sphairistike', he presented lawn tennis as an alternative to croquet. 'Croquet, which of late years has monopolised the attention of the public,' he said, 'lacks the healthy and manly excitement of 'Lawn Tennis'.' He used the attractive argument that 'the merest tyro can learn it in five minutes sufficiently well for all practical purposes,' and shrewdly enlisted the patronage of royalty and the nobility. Within a few years lawn tennis was an organised national and international sport. In 1875 the first national rules were drafted by the Marylebone Cricket Club which was responsible for real tennis. In 1877 the All-England Croquet Club became the All-England Croquet and Lawn Tennis Club, and the first lawn tennis championship was held at Wimbledon in the same year. The first Irish championship was held in 1879 and the first American one in 1880. The rules were successively revised until they were put into essentially their present form in 1883. The first ladies' championship attracted thirteen entrants in 1883. The Davis Cup series began in 1900.

The other sports met more specialised needs. Reference has been made to the rise of mountaineering and winter sports. The field sports were hardly affected by the new attitudes to sport in general. Foxhunting was by now unchallenged by hare-hunting. Shooting had reached high levels of destructiveness and sophistication as a result of further improvements in guns and the teachings of Colonel Peter Hawker who devoted most of his adult life to perfecting the techniques of the sport. Pheasant shooting became fashionable in the seventies and eighties after breech-loading came in, and vast sums were spent and incredible slaughter done by the new and the old rich. Between 1867 and 1900 Lord Ripon killed over 140,000 pheasants, nearly 100,000 partridges, 56,000 grouse, 30,000 rabbits, and nearly 28,000 hares, not to mention 11 tigers and two rhinoceroses.[40]

For reasons which remain obscure two of the manlier ball games – hockey and lacrosse – began among men but were largely taken over by women and girls. Hockey, a game of obscure origin, was reshaped during the sixties and seventies. The first national regulating body was set up in 1876 and the present one in 1886; the All-England Women's Hockey Association followed in 1891. As with Rugby Union the policy throughout has been that the game should be confined to amateurs. Lacrosse came from Canada and the English Lacrosse Association was formed as early as 1868, only a year after the Canadian national body. The revival of bowls began in Scotland, and in 1849 what is still substantially the present code of laws was adopted. The Scottish Bowling Association was not, however, formed until 1892. W. G. Grace after retiring from cricket took a prominent part in the establishment of an English national body in 1903. The first Oxford and Cambridge boat race – rowed for a monetary stake – was held in 1829, and Henley Regatta dates from 1839. Until 1861 the Wyfold Sculls were still rowed for a prize, but the Amateur Rowing Association (formed in 1882) was to be particularly rigorous on the question of amateurism: its rules excluded all 'menial or manual workers.' Polo was brought to England from India in 1869. Squash, which developed from a form of racquets played at Harrow, was referred to as a new game in 1890. Athletic sports in the sense the term is now used were almost unknown till the fifties and sixties: the Amateur Athletic Club, which was formed in 1866, excluded 'mechanics, artisans or labourers.'

Boxing and horse-racing were special cases. Boxing was held in almost religious regard by the muscular Christians. 'Learn to box', said Hughes in *Tom Brown's Schooldays*, 'as you learn to play cricket and football. Should you never have to use it in earnest, there's no exercise in the world so good for the temper, and for the muscles of the back and legs.' A few boxing clubs had come into being by the sixties, and the first amateur championship took place in 1867. Boxing was encouraged by the boys' clubs, and the enthusiasts who formed the Amateur Boxing Association in 1880 were fanatically opposed to professionalism. This was justified. Professional boxing had a bad reputation which was partly a legacy from prize-fighting and was partly due to the continued prevalence of corruption and other abuses. Much-needed cleansing operations began with the Queensberry rules in 1865, and were carried on by the National Sporting Club, which was formed in 1891.

Unlike prize-fighting horse-racing was never eclipsed. 'Very plebeian and very patrician' (as Cobbett said of Derby Day), it continued to enjoy aristocratic and mass support: – a reminder incidentally that Puritanism did not hold universal sway. But it was encumbered by a tradition of corrupt practices such as doping and the fixing of races in which even famous sportsmen like Squire Osbaldeston had been unashamedly involved. It was also alien to Victorian middle-class values because it was inseparably linked with gambling. The Jockey Club proceeded bravely with the task of reforming the Turf, and it was slowly restored to acceptability among the less puritanically minded of the respectable classes. Probably no single event contributed more to its rehabilitation than the victory of the Prince of Wales' horse Persimmon in the Derby of 1896.

There was no special significance in the fact that Victoria began her reign with a Proclamation for the Encouragement of Piety and Virtue, and for the Prevention of Punishment of Vice, Profaneness and Immorality. The State as such had only a subordinate part in enforcing the puritanical code of conduct during the Victorian period. Social disapproval and the pangs of individual conscience were the main sanctions against failure to conform to standards in which more or less everybody was indoctrinated from childhood. In this respect radical and free-thinking working men were often as orthodox as church and chapel-goers. Reading novels on Sunday and playing cards for money were offences not against the law but against conventions which it was almost as perilous to defy in respectable circles. When it came to tightening the law, however, the pressures for additional restrictions were usually counter-balanced by opposition from the vested interests and by the reluctance of politicians to add to the powers of the State or to alienate electors who saw no harm in a flutter or a Sunday excursion. Only minor changes were made in the Sunday observance laws. The problem of Sunday trading was not seriously tackled until the new century, and the Sunday Observance Act of 1782, which had been passed with the limited object of checking blasphemous meetings, was sufficiently elastic to cover all Sunday entertainments. The gambling laws were strengthened to take account of innovations such as the spread of betting shops in the 1840s, and those relating to prostitution in the eighties after an ill-fated experiment with licensing. Only the liquor laws – rendered ineffectual by the Acts of 1828 and 1830 – received radical overhaul. This was badly needed and tardily achieved. Despite the grave social evils due to drink this task was hardly begun until 1869 when Parliament once again brought all licensed premises under the control of the magistrates. It was made more difficult by opposition from the trade and by the extremism of many temperance reformers, and it was not substantially completed until the Balfour Act of 1904 and the drastic reduction of licensing hours during and after the First World War.

The puritanical code was sustained, replenished and in large measure policed by the churches and a multiplicity of voluntary organisations mostly with religious affiliations. They are exemplified by the Lord's Day Observance Society, and even better by the temperance societies which were well developed by the thirties especially in Scotland. At first they did not oppose drinking in moderation but they were soon advocating total abstention, and after the foundation of the United Kingdom Alliance in 1853, some of them began to press for prohibition or at least local option. Local option became the policy of the Liberal party in 1890 and would have become law but for the rejection of a Government Bill by the House of Lords in 1908. In this respect the Lords almost certainly reflected majority opinion more reliably than the Commons.

All responsible people agreed that drunkenness and other social evils must be curbed but it was increasingly recognised that restrictions were not enough and that they must be combined with steps to provide better facilities for holidays and recreations and to educate the masses to higher standards. Thomas Cook was only the first of a number of travel agents who went into the business because they saw holiday excursions as an alternative to drink: until at any rate recently Frame's maintained some of the restrictions on drinking which its founder imposed in 1881. Facilities for recreations were provided by many philanthropic bodies for broader social reasons. Most of this activity was directed towards children and young people. The clubs and settlements of the latter part of the century laid diminishing stress on direct religious instruction and more on sport and other recreations. Mechanics' institutes, night schools, university extension classes, Quintin Hogg's Polytechnics, were established not only for educational purposes but in order to take boys and men off the streets and out of the pubs. It often perplexed their organisers that they tended to attract clerks and teachers and craft apprentices rather than the poorer and less skilled. The right use of leisure, including attendance at night school, said a leaflet issued by the Nottingham school board, would lead to 'respect and happiness'. 'Degradation and misery' would result from making 'the wrong choice – idling about the streets in bad company, going into public houses or low places of amusement, forming bad habits.'[41] William Booth harnessed the popular love of music to the cause of evangelism. Cardinal Manning supported Sunday excursions. Andrew Carnegie gave nearly £2 million to the building of public libraries especially in Scotland. Charles Booth pioneered the objective investigation of leisure as well as of other social questions. Baden-Powell in the new century established the boy scouts and girl guides – a novel and imaginative attempt to tackle problems which the youth clubs had only imperfectly solved.

Legislation affecting recreations directly was mainly restrictive but the State groped towards a more positive role. A beginning was made in the forties with legislation safeguarding open spaces in the interests of popular recreation, and it became accepted as a national responsibility that women and children should be protected against excessive hours and inadequate holidays. From the 1840's onwards local authorities were variously empowered to provide parks and recreation grounds, museums, art galleries, libraries and swimming baths. Music and dancing were expressly excluded when in 1879 they were enabled to use public swimming baths for other 'healthy' recreations in winter, but this limitation was removed in 1899, and in 1907 they were permitted to subsidise music and dancing in public parks. It was implicit in the Bank Holidays Act of 1871 that Parliament was responsible for ensuring a national minimum of public holidays and in the Shops Act of 1912 that all, including adult male workers, should be entitled to a weekly half-holiday in addition to a weekly rest-day.

5

TOWARDS MASS LEISURE

After 1918 and more particularly after 1945 opportunities for recreation grew at an entirely unprecedented rate. This was due to increasing leisure, increasing wealth and rapid technological progress.

The increase in leisure was only partly the result of shorter working hours. The 48-hour week became normal for manual workers after 1918 but at least among men subsequent reductions in hours were not on the whole taken in curtailments of the working week. Though the nominal working week had been further reduced, actual working hours (including overtime) of adult male manual workers averaged 48.5 in 1959 and 47.0 in 1965. To this extent J. M. Keynes was right when he forecast in the *General Theory* (1936) that the great majority of people would prefer increased income to increased leisure.[42] This did not, however, mean that they were indifferent to additional leisure. One of the reasons for working longer than the basic week was to earn more to spend on holidays and recreations, and the collective preference was in general for other methods of increasing the amount of leisure. The weekend was extended by the adoption of the five-day week which spread rapidly after 1945, and high priority was given to annual holidays with pay. The Holidays with Pay Act of 1938, which accepted the principle of entitlement to at least a week's annual holiday with pay, endorsed what was already the minimum practice in much of industry. By 1967 at least two weeks had become general in addition to public holidays, and it was often exceeded.

A similar consensus showed the value which was attached to the winter holiday at Christmas. Between the wars professional football matches and greyhound races were held on Christmas Day, and the arrival of the postman was part of the ritual. By the middle sixties there were no Christmas Day posts and no public entertainments except broadcasting, and economic activity came more nearly to a standstill than on any other day in the year. The absence from work typically lasted two or three days, and longer when the Christmas holidays merged with the weekend ones. Even in Scotland deeply-seated objections to Christmas virtually disappeared after the second war, and Scotsmen largely took over the English Christmas without giving up their traditional New Year holidays.

About Sunday observance majority opinion was in two minds. The failure to modernise the law was due partly to the efficiency of the Sabbatarian lobby. Among other successes the Lord's Day Observance Society secured the defeat of official proposals for the Sunday opening of the British Empire Exhibition in 1924, theatres and music-halls during the second war, and the Festival of Britain Pleasure Gardens in 1951. But they were only able to do so because of the hold the traditional Sunday had on large numbers of people. It was not simply because of fear of Sabbatarian criticism that until 1960 the Football Association banned Sunday matches and penalised players who took part in them: in the same year the Wolfenden Committee on Sport, which dissociated itself from the views of the Lord's Day Observance Society, recommended against commercially organised events on Sunday and against the playing of Sunday games during the normal hours of worship.

The main obstacle to change was a facet of the popularity of the Sunday holiday; – the fear that it might be jeopardised by the spread of Sunday employment as a result of the freeing of Sunday amusements. Moreover, the inconvenience of the restrictions to the public was mitigated by increased Sunday opening of cinemas under the system of local option introduced in 1932, the gradual popularisation of Sunday broadcasting programmes, the use of devices like Sunday dancing and skating clubs to get round the law, and the proliferation of motor cars and motor bikes.

These developments in turn contributed to the further softening of traditional attitudes which had become marked by the sixties. Proposals in the fifties to reform the law and even to appoint a committee of enquiry had little support in Parliament but in 1961 the Government appointed the Crathorne Committee on the law on Sunday observance. Its report in 1964 showed that a remarkable shift of opinion had occurred but there was widespread agreement on the need to combine liberalisation with safeguards of the special character of Sunday as a day of rest and relaxation. Most of the Churches which gave evidence now favoured reform while many of the witnesses concerned with entertainments showed no great enthusiasm for change and agreed that the special character of Sunday should be preserved. The Committee followed the weight of the evidence and recommended almost total liberalisation of the Sunday entertainment laws except in respect of sports matches involving the payment of players and certain forms of public entertainment on Sunday mornings. What by the standards of only a generation before was a revolutionary document roused little interest and little controversy. A Bill based on it was introduced into the House of Lords by Lord Willis in 1966. It had not, however, passed into law when this book was completed.

The badly-needed reorganisation of the bank holidays to meet modern needs was delayed by religious difficulties connected with the date of Easter. Lubbock's initiative in 1871 was not followed by further action for nearly a century until in 1965 the August Bank Holiday was switched to the end of August and in 1967 the late Spring bank holiday was for the first time dissociated from Whitsun.

The effective growth in leisure cannot be measured solely or chiefly in reduced working hours and longer holidays. Other changes made a bigger contribution. Smaller families and the use of labour-saving devices freed time which was formerly devoted to household routine. People had more money to spend. Despite mass unemployment the standard of living improved between the wars, and faster still under full employment after 1945. Perhaps most important of all, accessibility to recreations was vastly increased by the breath-taking speed with which the mass media developed and the spread of the motor car for private and public transport.

Recreational reading grew at an astonishing rate. The popular newspapers built up their circulations by increasing the amount of space they devoted to entertainment, and the more serious papers slowly followed their example. The *Daily Mail* had reached two million by 1929. In the thirties Beaverbrook's *Daily Express* took the lead in sales after a savage circulation war with Odham's *Daily Herald* but both were soon outstripped by the tabloid *Daily Mirror* which had a daily circulation of over five million in 1966 as compared with nearly four million for the *Daily Express*. The Sunday papers, which could be read at greater leisure and provided even more entertainment, had bigger circulations still. The *Survey of Merseyside* noted in the thirties that in poorer families the Sunday paper often provided reading for most of the week. In the fifties the *New of the World* was taken by every second household. The *Times* crosswords, which began to provide breakfast-time recreation for dons and higher civil servant in the twenties: Beachcomber and William Hickey and Osbert Lancaster: the rise and fall of *Picture Post* – created in 1938 and liquidated in the fifties: the disappearance of the middlebrow magazine – symbolised by the death of the *Strand* in 1951: the prosperity of the radical and intellectual *New Statesman* which boasted that its readers began at the lighter end of the paper: the rise of the women's magazines (four had circulations exceeding a million in 1966): the launching of the Sunday magazine supplements in the sixties: – all these would have a place in a full account of recreational journalism since 1918.

Despite the rise in educational standards the reading of books as distinct from newspapers and magazines never became a major recreation among the masses or indeed of large sections of the upper and middle classes in Britain. There was none the less a fast growing market for books which were read mainly for amusement, and new techniques of writing, production and marketing were applied to its exploitation. Of reading in general Lord Eustace Percy as President of the Board of Education said in 1927 that 'nearly every one in this country already has the habit and has it very badly. It has been discovered that the greatest 'mind opiate' in the world is to carry the eye along a certain number of printed lines in succession'.[43] There was rather more to it than that. Millions of readers bought – or more often borrowed – books in order to escape into the fantasy worlds of best-selling novels, spy and crime stories, political and war memoirs, and science fiction. Allen Lane launched the paperback revolution in 1938, book clubs on the American model flourished particularly in the thirties, and the public libraries were transformed. They at last accepted the responsibility of catering for the lighter (though never the more lurid) tastes of the reading public, and their acceptance by all classes as a normal source of reading matter contributed after the second world war to the closure of the big chains of commercial libraries. By the sixties British public libraries were issuing about 500 million volumes a year: this was about double the number just after the war.

The twenties and thirties were the great age of the cinema. The introduction of talking pictures in 1928 added to the fantastic popularity it had already achieved, and the anxieties of some intellectuals who feared that sound would destroy its unique merits as an art were soon forgotten. Cinema attendances ultimately rose to an almost incredible peak of 30 million a week in 1947 but they were extremely sensitive to the spread of television. They were still running at an average of around 25 million in 1954: in 1965 the weekly average was just over 6 million.

The cinema met deep needs which were common to all classes and for that matter all races. It satisfied a universal craving for fantasy and escape. Vast sums were spent upon its exploitation. Films produced at fabulous cost to carefully contrived formulae were built round synthetically created stars who enjoyed world-wide fame. The death of Rudolph Valentino in 1926 evoked more emotion than a major earthquake disaster: in the thirties girls joined Garbo clubs and waved their hair in the style of Norma Shearer. The performances took place in the hypnotic environment of darkened interiors, plush luxury and organ music: the Granadas and Odeons which rose in the city centres symbolised the prosperity of the industry and the importance of the cinema in the life of the people.

Three facts largely shaped the early history of broadcasting in Britain, and their effects can still be seen. For technical reasons it was organised as a monopoly. Partly by accident it was placed under a public corporation. And until the second war it was dominated by the puritanical genius of the Scottish engineer John Reith (now Lord Reith) who was the chief executive first of the commercially controlled British Broadcasting Company which was formed in 1922 and then of the British Broadcasting Corporation which replaced it in 1927. The possibilities of the radio as a recreational medium were not fully recognised at first but within a few years it was second only to the cinema. Owners of wireless sets grew from about a million in 1925 to nearly 9 million in 1939. The B.B.C. launched the first regular public television service in the world in 1936 but owing to the war it was not fully established until the fifties. Between 1954 and 1966 the number of television licences increased from over 3 million to over 13½ million, and in 1955 a second and commercial network was set up under the supervision of a new public corporation, the Independent Television Authority.

Whereas the cinema brought people out, sound and television broadcasting kept them at home. For the first time in history everybody at his own fireside had access to almost every kind of professional entertainment – at high standards of performance, day in and day out, and at every level of taste from the esoteric Third Programme (introduced in 1946) to soap operas and all-in wrestling. As with the cinema there were at first resistances among the professional classes. They had scarcely become acclimatised to the wireless before they were faced with forests of TV aerials which foreboded the intrusion into their homes of even more dangerous distractions from serious pursuits for their children and themselves. Most succumbed.

The full consequences of the universalisation of television cannot yet be foreseen. More even than the radio it integrated entertainment with everyday life, and the home quickly replaced the cinema as the main focus of popular amusement, including spectator sport. Attendances at cinemas and sporting events suffered seriously but the fear that 'live' performances would be adversely affected was not in general realised. As had happened with the radio, new and bigger audiences were created for theatres and concert halls, amateur artistic and cultural activities were stimulated, reading and hobbies were encouraged. And while actual attendance at sporting events fell, the number of armchair spectators multiplied.

Because broadcasting was monopolistic it raised in an acute form the question of the responsibilities of the mass media to the community. Censorship did not present a serious problem. It was left to the two public broadcasting authorities: an independent board of censors as for films was unnecessary. By what criteria, however, should programme policy be settled? How should minority needs be safeguarded? Should the public be given what it preferred or should deliberate use be made of the medium to raise popular standards of taste? If so, whose standards should be inculcated? Nobody challenged the need to provide for minority audiences or the desirability of using broadcasting for educational purposes in the broadest sense. What was at issue was the policy which should be followed where entertainment programmes for mass audiences were concerned. With almost unquestioning support from educated opinion Reith unequivocally set out to improve standards of popular entertainment, with those prevailing among the professional classes as the yardstick. This policy was endorsed by the Beveridge and Pilkington Committees in 1951 and 1960, but it led to continuing tension both before and after 1945. Commercial programmes

– mainly of popular music – from Luxemburg and Normandy attracted big audiences in the thirties, and the decision to establish commercial television was influenced by the belief that the B.B.C. paid insufficient attention to popular wishes. The main reason for the popularity of the 'pirate' radio stations operating outside territorial waters in the sixties was the inability of the B.B.C. to satisfy the thirst of teenagers and housewives for popular music.

Sport in the main followed the pattern set in the nineteenth century. The cult of sport spread throughout the community, but it was gradually stripped of its worst extravagances: even in the public schools it had always had important critics. The levels of involvement ranged from idolisation of sporting heroes and total acceptance of sport as a self-sufficient objective to mild interest in major sporting events and participation in the football pools. But it was pervasive. In the early sixties national newspapers normally devoted between 10 and 20% of their space to sport (including racing), and its importance in the national culture was shown by the assimilation into everyday language of many phrases derived from games such as 'it's not cricket', 'play the game', 'stymied' and 'below the belt'. Yet as far as participation was concerned (including attendance as spectators) it remained a minority activity mainly of males and the young, and sport as distinct from physical training did not become a fully recognised part of school life in the State system until after the Education Act of 1944. Most people paid lip service to sport much as most people vaguely adhered to Christianity while reserving active participation in worship to special occasions. For others it was a major source of emotional and often aesthetic satisfaction.

How traditional the pattern had become is shown by the absence of change in the national events which aroused most public interest – the Cup Final, the Test matches, the Boat Race, the Derby, the Grand National, and the professional heavy-weight championship fights. Football (particularly soccer) and cricket (particularly in England) retained their ascendancy at least in general esteem. They were looked upon as 'national' sports and were especially valued as the main team games. There were about a million soccer players in the middle sixties, and spectators at League and Cup matches numbered about 30 million in a season.

Nor had there been any significant changes in the subtly adjusted social gradings which national snobbery had evolved. Attempts by the Headmasters Conference in the twenties and by many others then and later to arrest the tendency for soccer to be identified exclusively with the working classes met with only limited success, but it enjoyed a minor vogue amongst the intelligentsia in the fifties and sixties. In general those on both sides of the invisible social frontiers respected them. It was not simply that sports such as polo and yachting were in their nature monopolies of the rich. Lawn tennis and hockey, for example, remained middle-class games, and in England the same was true of golf, though as a 'national' game it was played widely by all classes in Scotland. It was reported in 1963 that sixth-formers at a Harrow secondary modern school gave up cricket and football for golf because 'golf is a social asset'. For reasons bound up with the class system cycle-racing, bowls, pigeon-racing and even coarse fishing continued on the other hand to be mainly associated with manual workers. Swimming was the chief example of an important sport which completely cut across class barriers, but this is only another way of saying that people of all classes shared a love of the water, and swimming was an indispensable means of locomotion.

There were few major innovations. Greyhound racing with a mechanical hare, which began at Manchester in 1926, was chiefly a vehicle for betting. In 1966, with about 12 million spectators, it was the most popular spectator sport next to soccer. Motor racing developed inevitably in the automobile age. Its various forms included dirt track racing (introduced from Australia in 1928) and 'go kart' racing (introduced from America after 1945): both preserved some of the excitement of high speeds without all the risks.

The most significant change was probably the relative decline in popularity of team games in favour of sports in which the competitive element was secondary and the main object was the exercise of skill. It was claimed in the sixties that fishing was the fastest growing sport: estimates of the number of anglers ranged from one to two million. There was a snobbish as well as probably a Freudian element in the growing popularity – especially with girls and women – of horse riding as a sport and a spectacle before and after the second war: it also no doubt represented a reaction against motorisation and urbanisation. Even hunting continued to flourish. There were as many fox-hunts as ever in the sixties despite the technological revolution in agriculture, and attacks by the League against Cruel Sports gained little support in a fanatically animal-loving country. Climbing, caving, skiing (increasingly in Scotland as well as abroad), fencing, judo, archery and above all sailing showed the same tendencies at work. The number of people sailing dinghies at weekends rose from an estimated 13,000 in 1950 to a quarter of a million in 1964.[44] Among indoor games, contract bridge, which had been invented in France and was descended from whist, became established in Britain in the thirties.

Other traditional recreations held their own. The public-houses slowly adapted themselves to changed drinking habits, the competition of the cinema and broadcasting, the spread of the motor car, and female emancipation. Attempts to introduce culture such as the 'poetry in pubs' movement launched in the thirties and the Tavern Concerts begun in 1944 understandably made little impression. But skilful publicity, improved amenities and the decline of drunkenness raised the social status of the pub and encouraged men to bring their wives and girl friends with them. Even so they continued to be principally male institutions (in interesting contrast with the churches) and old customs like perpendicular drinking and the segregation of customers according to income and class showed no signs of disappearing.

Contrary to the expectations of social reformers neither popular education nor growing prosperity checked the gambling habit. It was encouraged by the enterprise of gambling promoters and the decline of puritanical restraints. Measured by net expenditure it was, however, much less important than either of the major popular vices, drink and tobacco. The Royal Commission on Betting, Lotteries and Gaming estimated in 1951 that the net cost was about £44 million or well under 1% of the national income, and found no evidence that it had increased in volume since the twenties. Most working people saw no objection to gambling in principle, and majority views clashed with those of the powerful minorities who regarded it as a grave social evil. It was common ground that some controls were essential. The authorities responsible for law and order could not ignore the close association between gambling and the criminal world nor the consequences of widespread non-compliance with unenforceable restrictions.

National policies were inevitably ambivalent. Between the wars totalisator betting was placed under a public monopoly, and Winston Churchill imposed an abortive betting tax. Participation was forbidden in the Irish and other overseas sweepstakes which flourished because public sweepstakes were illegal in Britain. Newspaper competitions and football pools were regulated: after ready-money betting on football was banned in 1920, the pool promoters had brought themselves within the law again by collecting the wager a week after it was laid. This served to highlight the anomaly by which cash betting off the course (which was prevalent among working people) was illegal, whereas credit betting and cash betting on the course (the forms of betting mainly used by richer punters) were permitted. Changing attitudes in the postwar period were exemplified by the reintroduction of State lotteries in the form of premium bonds in the fifties – however modest this step may seem it would have been unthinkable even in the thirties – and by the revolutionary report which the Royal Commission presented in 1951. The object of gambling legislation, it recommended, should be to interfere as little as possible with individual liberty to take part in the various forms of gambling but to impose such restrictions as were desirable and practicable to discourage or prevent excess. Its realistic logic found general acceptance, and in 1960 legislation was passed which was intended to bring all gambling into the open under safeguards against abuse. It had consequences which its promoters had not anticipated. The street bookmaker disappeared with the legalisation of betting shops but the door was opened to commercially-organised bingo on a large scale and to a proliferation of casinos and clubs at which roulette, baccarat and other games were played for high stakes.

The pessimists who dwelt mainly on the pathological aspects of modern recreations or complained that they were unduly passive should have been reassured by the extraordinary popularity – particularly after the second war – of recreational activities in which the object was self-expression or self-improvement. They ranged from hobbies and the keeping of pets to the fine arts and the pursuit of learning. There were about 20 million non-professional gardeners in the middle sixties: surveys suggested that roughly one in three was keen, one moderately keen, and one unenthusiastic. At least half a million people were taking part in amateur dramatics, a similar number attended the Picasso exhibition at the Tate Gallery in 1960, and many millions of records of classical music were sold every year. Popular music and dancing flourished both before and after the second war, and unlike the serious arts and sport needed no public subsidies. Dancing appealed especially to young women and girls, but the Carnegie Trust's study of the eighteen plus age group between 1936 and 1938 found that many young men passed through a 'dancing mad' phase. It was not only that 'the search for a mate and dancing go hand in hand'. There was also connoisseurship. They demanded a high standard from the band and searched far and wide among foreign radio stations to 'satisfy their thirst for 'swing' and 'rhythm'.' After the war 'beat' and 'pop' groups in large numbers sprang up at the universities and public schools as well as in working class areas. Over 60 million gramophone records of a 'pop' type were produced in Britain in 1965. In the same period some six million people were going to public dances every week: 'olde tyme' dancing and the by now classical dances of the fox-trot age were popular among the middle-aged and elderly. There was a small but eager minority of folk and country dancers and Britain led the world in demonstration ball-room dancing.

Incalculable numbers engaged in what came to be known as 'do it yourself' activities – home decoration and improvement, looking after cars and domestic equipment, traditional female arts such as knitting and dressmaking. For many the satisfaction to be derived from creative effort and the exercise of skill was more important than the financial saving. Manufacturers and the mass media supplied the home craftsman with lavish advice, and his labours were lightened by inventions such as emulsion paints and cheap power tools. Home entertaining was stimulated by the spread of affluence and the motor car, and housewives and husbands applied the lessons about good food and wine which press, radio and television ceaselessly provided. Amateur gardening was revolutionised by new technological aids, advances in plant breeding and the dissemination of expert advice through the mass media. In amateur photography the cine camera and the colour film opened up new worlds. Nearly one household in two in 1965 kept a pet, with budgerigars slighty outnumbering cats and dogs, and the goldfish in his bowl was being ousted by exotic fish in thermostatically controlled tanks more apt for a technological age. Bird watching, amateur archaeology, flower arrangement, philately, these and many other praiseworthy pursuits grew in popularity. Well over two million people were attending evening classes in the sixties, most of them in subjects which were cultural and recreational rather than specifically vocational.

The automobile set the people free for leisure even more than the railway a century before – the motor bike, the charabanc, the bus and the coach no less than the private car. The number of private cars rose from under 200,000 in 1920 to over one million in 1930 and to nearly two million in 1939 but they did not come within the reach of most working people until the fifties and sixties. During the ten years from 1955 the figure more than doubled, and in 1965 the number of cars and motor cycles together amounted to nearly 11 million – roughly one in five of the population, men, women and children. Most of them were used primarily for pleasure: it was estimated that three-fifths of those taking annual holidays did so by car.

Less than half the population spent a single night away from home on holiday in 1938. In 1964 it was estimated that about 31 million people took an annual holiday away from home, and about 5 million more than one in the year. Most of the holiday-makers still went to the coasts of Britain. But increasing numbers – over 5 million in 1965 – went abroad, chiefly to Southern Europe and chiefly in search of the sun which even in the inter-war period had become the chief tourist magnet. And the range within which holiday travel was practicable was vastly extended by the development of air transport. New forms of holiday were invented and old ones adapted to modern needs. Youth hostels on the German model were developed by the Youth Hostels Association which was formed in 1930. Later in the thirties William Butlin created the modern British style of holiday camp. The chain of camps which he started in 1937 offered packaged holidays combining most of what his patrons looked for in a seaside holiday without the usual chores and inconveniences. He showed an understanding of popular psychology which was lacking among the intellectuals who laughed at his methods and complained that they were totalitarian in tendency. By the sixties one in twenty people spent their holiday in a holiday camp. Camping under canvas, which had hitherto been mainly associated with soldiers and boy scouts, and caravanning, which in prospect still roused romany visions, also spread fast after the second war, though less rapidly than on the Continent. They appealed to the love of the open air, the desire for independence and the masochistic delight in hardship which were part of the national tradition. In 1965 it was estimated that one in seven holiday-makers went on caravan holidays. Motels which were introduced from the United States and were spreading slowly in the sixties provided motorists with streamlined alternatives to the traditional type of hotel.

What determined the lines on which holidays and recreations developed in modern Britain? There is a sense in which the main trends can be said to have been inevitable, irreversible, and inherent in the social and economic conditions. It is not purely coincidental – or due to imitation – that they were similar in other industrialised countries with different cultural traditions and political systems. Examples are the spread of holidays with pay, the popularity of team games, the identification of national and local communities with the fortunes of representative teams, and the use of television as a major recreational medium. But a purely determinist view would not be justified. Within a broadly common international pattern there were important variations reflecting cultural differences, and important choices remained open to British people. It requires no sensitivity to distinguish between the British and Continental Sundays. Basket-ball and baseball did not take root here nor have cricket or so far soccer established themselves in the United States.

As far as Britain was concerned the Puritan tradition was a diminishing but still always an important factor in many of the choices which were made. Teetotalism declined, gambling became more respectable, Sunday observance less strict, attitudes towards other people's pleasures more and more relaxed. But puritanical tendencies were never much below the surface, and they were particularly strong among the opinion-making classes and persons in authority. And organised puritanism exerted an influence which was disproportionate to the number of its active sympathisers. There were periodical waves of anxiety about the moral state of youth, and nineteenth-century hysterics over the indecency of the waltz were recalled by middle-aged reactions to the charleston, the black bottom, rock 'n' roll and other popular dances which were supposedly erotic and were certainly exotic. Like their predecessors judges, politicians, leader-writers, ecclesiastics, correspondents to *The Times*, spoke for the public conscience. Not only gambling, drink and drugs but the cinema, television, novels and plays, dances (even the Lambeth walk), fun fairs, strip-tease, came under variously justifiable attack.

Pressure in the direction of restraint was exerted by the Churches and by voluntary bodies concerned with moral standards such as the temperance organisations, the Churches' Council on Gambling, and the Public Morality Council (which changed its name to the Social Morality Council in 1966 in order to mark the adoption of a broader and less negative approach in keeping with the times). The successes of the Lord's Day Observance Society showed the power of well organised minorities where majority opinion was apathetic and disunited. One of the objections which the Crathorne Committee saw in 1964 to local option on questions of Sunday entertainment was that the local option procedure for cinemas had been 'exploited by vociferous minorities...and aroused little interest among the general public.' Yet the differences were usually marginal in the last resort. Nobody disputed that the State must regulate certain fields – such as drink, gambling and indeed Sunday observance – and there was little support for total libertarians who wished to free Sunday amusements completely and to sweep away all forms of censorship. The national bias was puritanical. Most people were well enough satisfied with the compromises which were reached between licence and restraint. By and large only foreign visitors were dismayed by the torpor of the British Sunday, amazed by the liquor laws and depressed by the gloom which settled over the pleasure resorts by midnight.

It is hard to assess the effects of these activities but their object was openly restrictionist – to stop people from doing what they would prefer to do – and they had a considerable measure of success, particularly perhaps in delaying changes which would otherwise have occurred much earlier. Most of the other influences to which the public was subjected were unequivocally expansionist, and had the effect of stimulating the demand for particular recreations or for recreations in general.

There were of course the many interests which profited from recreations and holidays – directly in the case of, say, brewers, cinemas and holiday resorts, and indirectly in that of suppliers of recreational equipment and services such as catering and transport. They used modern publicity and selling methods to extend their markets and hold their own against competitive recreations. Where necessary – as, for example, with the brewers and the bookmakers – they organised to defend themselves against hostile critics. There was much criticism of commercialism in sport and other recreations. It was sometimes justified and usually misdirected. Evils such as philistinism and debasement of taste were due at least as much to popular preference as to the profitmaking agencies which sought to cater for it. Business interests either followed or tried to anticipate popular choice but the last word rested with the public, and the Government and Parliament could and did intervene where the wider interests of the community were thought to suffer. Because of declining cinema attendances in the fifties and sixties the cinema interests promoted bingo and ten-pin bowling: it lay with the public whether they took on. Industry was helping to finance professional golf, horse-racing and first-class cricket in the sixties: there was criticism but the responsibility for accepting the help lay ultimately with the governing bodies of the sports. The pirate radio stations discovered an unsatisfied demand for marathon 'pop' programmes: in this instance the Government decided that the need should be met not by them but by the B.B.C.

Less noticed than the promotional activities of commercial interests were those consciously or unconsciously engaged in by the participants in the different recreations. In the sixties there were about 300 governing bodies in the field of sport, and there must have been at least as many national organisations which were concerned with the promotion and coordination of other recreational pursuits. They were in turn the apex of hundreds of thousands of regional and local bodies. Through its constituents the National Federation of Anglers embraced an individual membership of 400,000 in 1966: and the thousand or so societies which belonged to the National Federation of Music Societies were only a small proportion of the total. Each of these bodies – every national organisation, every branch or individual club, indeed every active member – was a focus of enthusiasm and effort directed towards the propagation and perpetuation of the particular recreation. The governing bodies for the major sports took a special interest in public relations and in the indoctrination and training of the younger generation, and, as they settled the rules and in large measure the conditions under which the sport could be pursued, they exercised powers over the public unusually sweeping for private organisations. They did not hesitate to use their authority where questions of policy and public relations arose. The Football Association proscribed organised Sunday football until 1960, and set its face against women's football: players who helped women's teams in the sixties were warned that they might be banned from games within the F.A.'s jurisdiction. In a famous case between the wars the Rugby Football Union refused to recognise an athletic bishop who many years before had played in Rugby League. The M.C.C. sponsored Sunday matches in the sixties in order to regain some of the popularity of cricket with spectators. The Jockey Club and the British Boxing Board of Control set and enforced high standards for participation in horse-racing and professional boxing.

Public attitudes were also affected by the activities of many other voluntary organisations. In some the interest was secondary or incidental to other objectives. This was true, for example, of the trade unions which as part of their wider functions worked for better holidays and for higher pay to those forced to work at holiday-times, and of the many societies which fought for the preservation of amenities – for causes such as the protection of coast and countryside, the establishment of national parks and nature reserves, the preservation of commons and footpaths and historic buildings. Churches, clubs, welfare organisations, provided recreational facilities to keep young people off the streets, to offset the loneliness of the aged, to maintain the morale of the unemployed in the thirties. Women's institutes, townswomen's guilds, and community centres met recreational among other needs. Humanitarians formed the League for the Prohibition of Cruel Sports in 1926: Lady Summerskill and others crusaded against boxing in the fifties and sixties.

Other bodies such as the Youth Hostels Association, the Workers Travel Association (founded in 1921) and the National Playing Fields Association (founded in 1925) existed wholly or mainly for the provision of recreational facilities which they believed to be socially beneficial.

The role of the State was transformed, mainly after 1945. In part this was a by-product of wider policies involving increasing intervention in social and economic life. Usually acting through the local authorities, the State assumed new responsibilities for regulating recreational activities which might endanger safety, health and amenities. New or increased powers were taken to deal with such matters as litter, the location and regulation of holiday camp and caravan sites, holiday traffic and advertising in the countryside. Decisions in fields such as town and country planning, taxation of consumer expenditure, development areas, exchange control, and public transport affected recreations like everything else and involved or implied judgments between recreational and other activities and between different uses of leisure. The theatre and sport were first subject to, and then exempted from the entertainments tax: particular holiday resorts gained from the preferential treatment of development areas: aid was given to horse-racing in support of the bloodstock industry. Other forms of recreation were discouraged as an indirect result of such measures as exchange restrictions and the closing of branch railway lines.

The State also assumed more positive responsibilities for the planning and development of holidays and recreations – for the most part rather later than in comparable Continental countries. The turning point came shortly before the second war. The Physical Training and Recreation Act of 1937 extended the powers of the Government and local authorities to make grants to voluntary bodies such as the Central Council of Physical Recreation. What was perhaps most significant was that it was only as a result of public pressure that recreation was given equal weight to physical training. The Act had been preceded by the National Fitness Campaign launched with £2 million, and the Council had been set up as a coordinating agency in 1935 as the Council of Recreative Physical Training. It was only after the Bill was introduced that it was amended to refer specifically to recreation and the title of the Council was changed. Aneurin Bevan denounced it on the ground that the desire to play was its own justification and there was no need to invoke the national well-being.

The next important step was also forced on the Government. The Holidays with Pay Act of 1938 resulted from the initiative of another Labour member, Ellen Wilkinson: as we have seen, in spirit if not in terms it established the right to holidays with pay for employed persons. A new phase in State patronage of the arts began with the creation of the Council for the Encouragement of Music and the Arts to promote war-time morale in 1939, and with the establishment of its peace-time successor, the Arts Council, in 1946 as an independent chartered body supported from public funds. In 1948 local authorities were given the power to incur greatly increased expenditure on the provision of entertainments. Post-war Governments made on the whole ineffectual attempts to encourage the staggering of summer holidays, but the reorganisation of bank holidays in the sixties was a major advance in the planning of public holidays in the national interest. Anxiety about the state of youth led to the appointment of the Albemarle Committee in 1958 and its report in 1961 to the expansion and reorganisation of the Youth Service. The administration of public libraries was rationalised under the Public Libraries and Museums Act of 1964 after the Roberts report of 1959. The report of the Wolfenden Committee on Sport and the Community (1960), which had been appointed not by the Government but by the Central Council of Physical Recreation, led to increasing governmental interest and expenditure on sport under both the Conservative and Labour Governments, and in 1965 effect was given to the recommendation of the Committee that a Sports Council should be set up. The appointment in 1964 and 1965 of Ministers in the Department of Education and Science with specific responsibilities for sport and the arts – Mr. Dennis Howell as 'Minister for Sport' and Miss Jennie Lee as 'Minister for the Arts' – was not only indicative of the growing importance which the Government attached to both subjects. It also reflected the widespread sense that these were forms of recreation of special benefit to the community which more than others justified governmental support.

'*Vers une civilisation du loisir?*' This question was asked in 1962 by Joffre Dumazedier, one of the leading sociologists now studying problems of leisure. It is not a new concept. 'We are unleisurely in order to have leisure,' wrote Aristotle,[46] and many civilisations have been based on the pursuit of leisure by a privileged minority. What would be new would be a civilisation of which a major feature was the enjoyment of substantial leisure by more or less everybody. There is every reason for fearing that taking the world as a whole it is a remote dream. If things are well ordered it may be within the grasp of the more advanced societies in a generation or two.

To speculate on how it might be brought about in Britain and what form it might take is not the business of this book. It is impossible to sum up an unfinished story and not much use wondering about the outcome when the plot is still being unwound. But past experience does make it possible to predict some of the chief questions which future planners in the field of recreations will have to ask themselves. What goals should be set and what standards – ethical, cultural, aesthetic, social – should be encouraged? In what if any circumstances should those of an élite be imposed on the common man or those of the majority on minorities? And what controls will be unavoidable in order to safeguard the freedoms of others and to protect the individual from himself? How in short can liberty and discipline be reconciled?

NOTES AND REFERENCES

To save space I have only given references if there are specific reasons for doing so. In general I have not thought it essential where the information is obtainable in standard authorities and works of reference, the source (though not necessarily the precise reference) is clear from the text, or the point is unimportant. I will do my best to answer queries from readers who are handicapped by the lack of complete references and wish to follow up particular points in their own research.

1 H. S. Bennett and G. S. Homans are the main authorities – see *Bibliographical Note*.
2 E. F. Salzman, *Building in England down to 1540* (1952), 63-5. The ordinances refer to Calais, but there is no reason to doubt that they were in a standard form.
3 See especially G. T. Salusbury, *Street Life in Medieval England* (2nd. ed. 1948) and Salzman, *op. cit.* and other works.
4 Gwyn A. Williams, *Medieval London* (1963), 317. All population estimates are highly speculative for this period but we are only concerned with an order of magnitude.
5 W. E. Mead, *The English Medieval Feast* (1931), 33.
6 Frederick Harrison, *Medieval Man* (1947), 108-9.
7 G. G. Coulton, *The Medieval Village* (1926), 422-3.
8 J. C. Cox, *Church-wardens' Accounts* (1913) contains much interesting information about church ales.
9 R. L. Greene (ed.), *The Early English Carols* (1935), 355.
10 *Ibid*, 261.
11 Chabham's instructions have been widely quoted – see, for example, E. K. Chambers, *The Medieval Stage* (1903), II, 262-3, which gives them in the original Latin.
12 *The Master of Game*, ed. W. A. and R. B. Grohmann (1909), was the first book on hunting in English. It was written by Edward, second Duke of York, but was largely translated from the French of Gaston de Foix.
13 This information about the late arrival of the rabbit in Britain comes from Elspeth M. Veale, *The English Fur Trade in the Later Middle Ages* (1966).
14 A. L. Rowse, William Shakespeare (1963), quoting C. F. E. Spurgeon, *Shakespeare's Imagery* (1935), 110.
15 Cit. W. B. Whitaker, *Sunday in Tudor and Stuart Times* (1933), 34.
16 Cit. Christopher Hill, *Society and Puritanism in Pre-Revolutionary England* (1964), 125.
17 *The Vindication of Christmas* (1653).
18 Cit. J. E. B. Mayor (ed.), *Cambridge under Queen Anne* (1925), 208.
19 A. S. Turberville (ed.), *Johnson's England* (1952 ed.), I, 185.
20 Marion Lochhead, *The Scots Household in the Eighteenth Century* (1948), 288.
21 Henri Misson, cit. Reginald Lennard, *Englishmen at Rest and Play* (1931), 52.
22 *The English Magazine*, December 1737, cit. A. Barbeau, *Life and Letters at Bath in the XVIIIth Century* (1904), 49.
23 *Catherine Hutton's Letters*, ed. C. Hutton Beale (1891), 150.
24 H. G. Graham, *Social Life of Scotland in the Eighteenth Century* (1928), 96.
25 According to some experts the Darley Arabian may eventually become the common male ancestor of every thoroughbred.
26 Lochhead, *op cit.*, 172.
27 Cf. Herrick's poem 'Stoolball'.
      If thou, my dear, a winner be
      At trundling of the ball,
      The wager thou shalt have, and me.
28 R. S. Holmes, *The History of Yorkshire County Cricket 1833-1903*, (1904), 10.
29 Edward Hughes, *North Country Life in the Eighteenth Century. The North East, 1700-1750* (1952), 366.
30 M. D. George, *London Life in the Eighteenth Century* (1925), 287.
31 Sidney and Beatrice Webb, *History of Liquor Licensing in England* (1903), 149.

32 *Ibid.*, 150.

33 *Change for 'The American Notes'* (1843) by 'An American Lady'.

34 House of Commons on the Factories Bill, 3 March, 1847: *Hansard*, vol. *XC*, col. 774. I am indebted to Mr E. Royston Pike for this reference.

35 In 1872 the Great Northern Railway introduced three days holiday with pay for employees with at least a year's service. (Philip S. Bagwell, *The Railwaymen*, (1963), 66). This is the earliest example of paid holidays in industry of which I am aware. No doubt there were earlier ones. I should be glad to hear from anybody who comes across earlier examples.

36 Alfred Marshall, *Principles of Economics* (ed. C. W. Guillebaud, 1961), I, 694.

37 The evidence for this interpretation of the origin of the modern Father Christmas was first published in an unsigned article of mine, 'Gifts and Stockings. The Strange Case of Father Christmas' in *The Times*, 22 December, 1956.

38 Philip Snowden, *The Living Wage* (1912), 66.

39 O. L. Owen, *The History of the Rugby Football Union* (1955), 40.

40 F. M. L. Thompson, *English Landed Society in the Nineteenth Century* (1963), 340.

41 David Wardle, 'The Nottingham School Board's Experiments in Vocational Education'. *The Vocational Aspect*, Spring 1965, Vol. XVII, No. 36, 36.

42 J. M. Keynes, *The General Theory of Employment, Interest and Money* (1936), 326.

43 Cit. Q. D. Leavis, *Fiction and the Reading Public* (1965 ed.), 55.

44 The statistics about participation in different recreations in this chapter have been drawn from many sources – official figures, Parliamentary debates, interested groups – and are in some cases only informed estimates. Unless otherwise clear from the context they should be treated with reserve except as indications of orders of magnitude. I am particularly indebted to the C.O.I.'s official handbook *Britain*.

45 Joffre Dumazedier, *Vers une Civilisation du Loisir?* (Paris, 1962).

46 This quotation from Aristotle was used as a text by Josef Pieper in *Leisure. The Basis of Culture* (1962).

BIBLIOGRAPHICAL NOTE

Joseph Strutt's great pioneer work *The Sports and Pastimes of the English People* (1801, revised and ed. J. C. Cox, 1903) continues to be an indispensable and often unacknowledged source of information about the history of recreations. The best treatment of the subject as part of a general social history will be found in G. M. Trevelyan's *English Social History* (many eds.): it is also dealt with well in R. J. Mitchell and M. D. R. Leys, *A History of the English People* (1950). It is impossible to list the many specialised social histories which contain more or less extensive references to recreations. Among innumerable others they include the standard works of writers such as G. G. Coulton, M. Dorothy George, the Hammonds, L. F. Salzman and A. S. Turberville and standard compendia like *Medieval England, Shakespeare's England, Johnson's England, Early Victorian England* (ed. G. M. Young, 1934) and *Edwardian England 1901-1014* (ed. Simon Nowell-Smith, 1964). Some of the most useful material is to be found in books dealing with particular areas, institutions and even families and individuals: the Notes and References contain a few examples out of many. H. D. Traill's *Social England* has not worn well. Secondary material on holidays except Sundays is jejune. H. S. Bennett, *Life on the English Manor* (1937) and G. C. Homans, *English Villagers of the Thirteenth Century* (1941) are useful for the Middle Ages. For later periods I have mainly relied on my own *The Englishman's Holiday* (1947) both on the extent of holidays and the way they were used. *The Medieval Stage* (1903) and other works by E. K. Chambers are indispensable on medieval holiday-making, and for later periods there is an extensive literature on life at the spas and seaside resorts. Of the many books dealing wholly or partly with Sunday observance Christopher Hill, *Society and Puritanism in Pre-Revolutionary England* (1964), is particularly illuminating and stimulating: it throws new light on the evolution of Sunday and other holidays during a critical period. Others to which I am much indebted are W. B. Whitaker, *Sunday in Tudor and Stuart Times* (1933) and *The Eighteenth-Century English Sunday* (1948), W. P. Baker's essay in *Englishmen at Rest and Play* (ed. Reginald Lennard, 1931), and the relevant section in Owen Chadwick, *The Victorian Church* (1965). There are many and usually repetitive histories of the English Christmas but they tend to be anecdotal and antiquarian in approach, and I have drawn mainly on my own researches, some of the results of which have been published in *The Times, History Today* and *New Society*.

I can only mention a few of the many histories of particular recreations: most of them have been written by addicts or journalists rather than by qualified historians. Among the best of those dealing with sports are H. S. Altham and E. W. Swanton, *A History of Cricket* (4th ed. 1948) and H. S. Altham, *A History of Cricket*, Vol. I, (1962); George T. Burrows, *All About Bowls* (n.d.); Geoffrey Green, *The History of the Football Association* (1953); Morris Marples, *A History of Football* (1954), which is noteworthy for an objectivity of approach unusual in most books about sport; and O. L. Owen, *The History of the Rugby Football Union*, (1955). Others which are valuable include J. D. Aylward, *The English Master of Arms* (1956), Lord Aberdare, *The Story of Tennis* (1959), R. Browning, *A History of Golf* (1955), Edmund Burke, *The History of Archery* (1958), Patrick Chalmers, *The History of Hunting* (1936) and *Racing England* (1939), Hylton Cleaver, *A History of Rowing* (1957), F. H. Cripps-Day, *The Tournament* (1918), J. B. Salmond, *The Story of the R. and A.* (1956), the Earl of Harewood and others, *Flat Racing* (1940), Viscount Knebworth, *Boxing* (1946). *Studies presented to F. M. Powicke* (1948) contains an important essay by N. Denholm-Young, 'The Tournament in the Thirteenth Century'. Conspicuous gaps include comprehensive histories of falconry and fishing. Chess and other board games are well served by three masterly works by H. J. R. Murray, *A History of Chess* (1913), *A History of Board Games other than Chess* (1952), and *A Short History of Chess* (1963).

Eating and drinking as recreations deserve more attention than they have received from historians but W. E. Mead, *The English Medieval Feast* (1931) is an important exception. On the history of drink as a social problem I have made use of S. and B. Webb, *The History of Liquor Licensing in England principally from 1700 to 1830* (1903), G. E. G. Catlin, *Liquor Control* (1931) and Hermann Levy, *Drink* (1957). There is surprisingly little about the history of gambling as such. J. Ashton, *The History of Gambling in England* (1898) is superficial but there is useful historical material in the *Reports* of the Royal Commissions on Lotteries and Betting (1931) and Betting, Lotteries and Gaming (1951).

I have used standard authorities for music, dancing and the drama. Asa Briggs, *The History of Broadcasting in the United Kingdom*, the first two volumes of which (1961 and 1965) go down to the war, is the standard work in its field. For the cinema in Britain there is the unfinished *History of the British Film* by Rachael Low (and Roger Manvell for the first volume), the third volume of which (1950) has reached 1918. Otherwise the material on these subjects is voluminous but fragmentary. The literature on the press is vast. Of special relevance to this book are R. D. Altick, *The English Common Reader, A Social History of the Mass Reading Public 1800-1900* (1957), Louis James, *Fiction for the Working Man 1830-1850* (1963), Q.D. Leavis, *Fiction and the Reading Public* (1932), R. K. Webb, *The British Working Class Reader 1790-1948* (1955), and R. Williams, *Culture and Society 1780-1850* (1958) and other works.

On attitudes to leisure and recreations ecclesiastical and educational histories are often valuable, particularly the extensive literature about Puritanism. More general works which in their various ways I have found especially interesting and stimulating include Ford K. Brown, *Fathers of the Victorians* (1961), S. G. Checkland, *The Rise of Industrial Society in England 1815-1885* (1964), Christopher Hill's already mentioned *Society and Puritanism* and other works, John E. Mason's fascinating *Gentlefolk in the Making* (1935), which comprehensively analyses 'courtesy' literature between 1531 and 1714, G. E. Mingay, *English Landed Society in the Eighteenth Century* (1963), L. Radzinowicz, *History of the English Criminal Law* (1948 etc.), *Lawrence Stone, The Crisis of the Aristocracy 1558-1641* (1965), E. P. Thompson, *The Making of the Englisch Working Class* (1963), and F. M. L. Thompson, *English Landed Society in the Nineteenth Century* (1963). Invaluable light is thrown on the emergence of modern sport in the many books on the Victorian public schools, in particular D. Newsome, *Godliness and Good Learning* (1961). Changing attitudes to physical education are ably analysed in P. C. McIntosh, *Physical Education in England since 1800* (1952) and in contributions by the same writer and others to F. E. Leonard and G. B. Aflick, *A Guide to the History of Physical Education* (1947), and J. G. Dixon and others, *Landmarks in the History of Physical Education* (1957). Peter Fryer, *Mrs. Grundy. Studies in English Prudery* (1963), is amusing as well as informative on continuing puritanical protest. E. S. Turner, *All Heaven in a Rage* (1964), covers inter alia the humanitarian revolt against blood sports. Richard Hoggart, *The Uses of Literacy* (1957), is invaluable to the student of popular leisure today. Little has been published about the role of the State and local authorities in the field of recreations: S. K. Ruck, *Municipal Entertainment and the Arts in Greater London* (1965), is a welcome and admirable exception.

Leisure activities have been dealt with more or less adequately in most social surveys since Charles Booth's survey of London Life and Labour, and there have been a few special studies such as the Carnegie Trust's *Disinherited Youth, 1936-1939* and Michael Dower's Civic Trust survey *Fourth Wave. A Challenge of Leisure* (1965), which looked ahead to the future. Geoffrey D. M. Block, *Britons on Holiday* (1963), published by the Conservative Political Centre, contains a useful review of the position then. The most ambitious survey of *English Life and Leisure* – by B. Seebohm Rowntree and G. R. Lavers (1951) – is disproportionately concerned with the pathological aspects. *Patterns of British Life* (1950) published by the Hulton Press, and the annual C.O.I. publication *Britain. An Official Handbook* are indispensable quarries of information on leisure pursuits.

Relevant sociological works of which I have made use include Thorsten Veblen's classic *The Theory of the Leisure Class*, still stimulating though only partly convincing, and well-known books by Nels Anderson, Henry Durant, G. Friedmann, Geoffrey Gorer, J. Huizinga, Josef Pieper and F. Zweig. Most of the original thinking on the sociological problems of leisure as such now seems to be taking place abroad, and I should like to refer especially to three books which I have found particularly stimulating: Joffre Dumazedier, *Vers une Civilisation du Loisir?* (Paris, 1962 and published in England as *Towards a Society of Leisure*, 1967), Georges Magnane, *Sociologie du Sport* (Paris, 1964), and David Riesman, *Abundance for What?* (1964). As for work here, I look forward to the forthcoming publication of N. Elias and Eric Dunning, *The Making of Football. A Sociological Study*, which was foreshadowed by the authors' article 'Dynamics of groups sports with special reference to football' in the *British Journal of Sociology*, December 1966.

For the inter-war and post-war periods I have drawn extensively on official publications and newspapers and my own memory and experience.

Some of the subjects covered in this book are also referred to in other volumes in this series – the rise of the holiday resorts in Geoffrey Martin, *The Town*, the place of sport and other recreations in education in Malcolm Seaborne, *Education*, and the export of British games and ideas on sport in Jack Simmons, *Britain and the World*.

1 Entertainment fit for a king in Anglo-Saxon England. Though especially associated with the Welsh and the Irish, the harp was also popular among the Anglo-Saxons. In the 7th century, Caedmon was the only man on an estate of Whitby Abbey who could not play it. The ancient art of juggling – here with both knives and balls – was a favourite medieval entertainment. Hence 'jongleur' as a generic term for minstrels.

SEPTEMBER HABET

XVI   H F
V   O I G III M

2 A September hunting scene in the 11th century when the wild boar was still plentiful in the many forests. Despite the protection of the forest laws it was almost extinct by the 13th century. The boar also had a symbolic significance which was expressed in the boar's head carols and ceremonies of the later Middle Ages and in the popularity of brawn as a Christmas dish down to the 19th century.

3 Anglo-Saxon dinner party. Eating and drinking in congenial company has always been a major recreation, and majority opinion has usually been tolerant towards the sin of gluttony on festive occasions. Many other examples of feasting as a recreation will be found among later illustrations.

4 The Normans brought chess to Scotland, and there was a carver of chessmen at Kirkcudbright in the 12th century. These walrus-ivory chessmen, which are part of a collection found on the island of Lewis in 1831, may date from the same period but they are probably Icelandic. They represent king, queen, knight and bishop. (See also pl. 31)

5 A king and a lady playing (and apparently arguing over) a board game, probably 'tables', c.1340. Eight varieties of 'tables' – the medieval name for backgammon – were recorded in England in about 1300. A race game played with dice, it was one of the chief gambling games of medieval Europe. Ludo, which was invented in the late 19th century, belongs to the same family. (See also pl. 48, 79)

6 Aristocratic ladies occasionally hunted, and, as this 14th-century illustration shows, they sometimes hawked. But they did not usually take part in their husbands' outdoor recreations. (See also pl. 34, 96)

7 Club ball (14th century) was probably a precursor of cricket: an earlier reference occurs in a court case of 1293. The striped shirt should not be regarded as an ancestor of the football jersey.

8 Hockey in the 14th century? Though a game called hockey was played in late medieval Ireland, it would be unwise to jump to this obvious conclusion. The origins of the modern game as it developed in the 19th century are obscure. (See also pl. 111)

9 Kayles (14th century) was one of various forms of skittles which were popular in the Middle Ages, were played for money, and were condemned from time to time by Church and State. In this version a club was used to knock the 'kayles' or ninepins down. Ten-pin bowling (pl. 153) is a remotely related modern pastime.

10 The romanticised treatment of the national sport by this 14th-century artist contrasts with his cold look at the dice-play which distracted so many Englishmen from the patriotic duty of practising with the long bow (see also pl. 41, 69). Losing his shirt was already part of the price the gambler might have to pay for his addiction. Or was it a hot day?

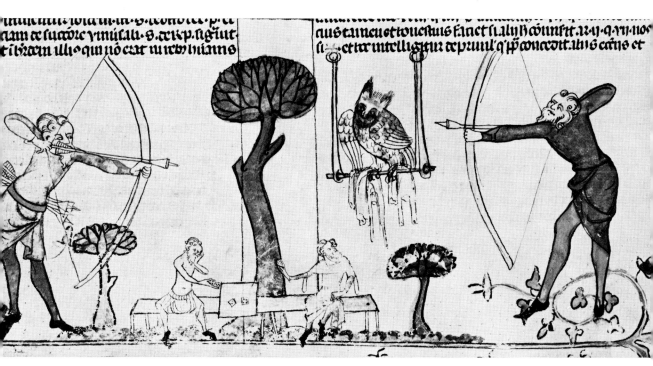

11 12 Many medieval games must have disappeared without trace. Of others nothing is known except no longer intelligible names or elusive glimpses to which no names can be attached. There is no obvious modern parallel to the 14th century game depicted in pl. 11 and described in the British Museum's notes on the Luttrell Psalter as 'cylindrical object to be tossed'. There are present-day children's games which resemble pl. 12 – 'seizing object on small mound with teeth', and it is similar in principle to ducking for apples at Hallowe'en parties in the 18th and 19th centuries. Using only his mouth the player had to get an apple out of a tub of water.

13 Described by the British Museum as 'pitch-in-the-hole' (14th cent.). Is it marbles?

14 'Water poured into funnel in man's mouth', *c.* 1340. Was this a game or a parlour trick or minstrel's act? Water – or at any rate a liquid – is being poured into the funnel, and presumably the man on his back has to blow it back again. But with what object? 'Evidently a game', says the British Museum with some lack of conviction, and with greater confidence a 'doubtful amusement'.

15 A bear-baiting, *c.* 1340. Animal-baiting was of ancient origin, and it was not confined to bears. Bull-baiting (pl. 25), cock-fighting and cock-throwing were popular, and there are references to fights between boars and to the baiting of horses by dogs. The man on the right is presumably the bear-ward.

grant duel a chafam que nul nel pi
Qui les uoir ne fe puet deplorer att
dr tant fort le regretent que nus ne
l trois garte le cors ams nele volt guer

les gens de jnde fount
xaudie pour lur Roy

16 Illustrations 16-22 come from the famous Flemish manuscript of the Romance of Alexander (*c.* 1340), which is accepted by scholars as applicable to England. Though probable, it is not, however, certain that there were puppet shows in medieval England, and any resemblance to the Punch and Judy show is mainly coincidental. The Punch and Judy show as such dates from the late 18th century (pl. 93). Performing bears were very popular, and other animals which minstrels took round with them, either as performers or as exhibits, included apes, dogs, horses, camels and even lions. For a sad reminiscence of the medieval performing bear see pl. 121.

17 Mummers *c.*1340. The 'mumming', 'guising' and masking characteristic of medieval folk dances and 'plays' looked back to prehistoric fertility rites and forward to the theatre, the masque, the pantomime and the fancy dress ball. (See also pl. 38, 92, 105)

Que oifeleur ne font menus oifiaus a glu

18 Women playing bowls. Their attitudes and gestures suggest a strong similarity of mood to the modern game. What appears to be the equivalent of the modern 'jack' was in use. (See also pl. 94, 130)

19-22 A series of illustrations depicting forms of fighting which were popular as recreations in the 14th century.

19 Fighting with cudgel and shield and on pick-a-back.

20 Moveable quintain. If the tilter does not move smartly after hitting the target, it will swing round and hit him.

21 Fixed quintain. Here the risk is of being knocked off the wooden horse.

22 Water quintain. And here of being tipped into the water.

23 Picking flowers, 14th century. It is easy to exaggerate the importance in medieval recreations of drunken merriment, violent sports and strange rituals. Medieval people also enjoyed simpler pastimes such as taking country walks, cultivating their gardens, keeping pets, reading and being read to, catching butterflies and picking flowers.

24 Swimming, said Sir Thomas Elyot in 1531, had not been 'of long time much used, especially among noblemen'. It was 'right profitable in extreme danger of wars', but there was 'some peril in the learning thereof'. Yet due precautions were evidently taken by some 14th-century instructors. (See also pl. 33)

25 Bull-baiting, 14th cent. (See also pl. 90)

26 Sword play, 14th cent. Stow in the 16th century called this 'the ancient English fight of sword and buckler'. By then it was threatened by the rise of rapier and dagger and of fencing in the Italian style.

place. yis speres born before hym . Then thaire of speres to therle Victau & worshipfully
fynysshed : after went they togedre w a poer , and if the sude Galuo suld nor the
sonner erud peas: if Randolf sore wonnded in the lifte shuldre hadde ben
titterly shynne in the folde .

27 Hand-to-hand combat. By the late 15th century the tournament was a highly organised spectator sport with varied
programmes and complex rituals in which the ladies took an important part.

28 Fools, clowns and jesters have always had an ambivalent role in social life, classically illustrated in Shakespeare's plays. The earliest reference to 'fools' at Court occurs in the 12th century. By the 14th they were common in noble and episcopal households, and they were to be found in May games and other popular festivities.

29 This vivid representation in a misericord at Gloucester Cathedral whets the appetite for better information about medieval football than is provided by ordinances, Court proceedings and the denunciations of monks and moralists. But is it football?

30 Playing-cards probably entered England in the late 14th century. By the middle of the next century they were sufficiently popular for card games except during the Christmas season to be banned in 1461 and for the importation of playing cards to be forbidden on protectionist grounds in 1463. Supplies continued, however, to come from France and the Netherlands for many years. These French cards show the continuity between medieval and modern design. (See also pl. 48, 91)

31 The second book printed by Caxton was *The Game of Chess* – his own translation from a French version of the famous 13th-century work by the Lombard monk Jacobus de Cessolis. De Cessolis drew political and other morals from chess, and judging from the number of surviving manuscripts his book rivalled even the Bible in popularity.

32 Henry VIII reading in his bedchamber. The 'full man' of the Renaissance found recreation in study as well as in sport and the arts. Elizabeth I regularly read Greek with Roger Ascham.

33 Everard Digby's *De Arte Natandi* (1587) was the first book on swimming published in England: an English translation appeared in 1595. He made an ingenious use of illustration as a teaching aid: the various strokes were shown in different insets imposed on the same river scene.

34 George Turberville's *Booke of Faulconrie* (1575), of which this is the frontispiece, was the first of three major books on the subject to be published between 1575 and 1620. It was largely reproduced from French medieval works. Simon Latham's *Falconry* (1615) and Edmund Bert's *An Approved Treatise of Hawkes and Hawking* (1619) were more original.

35 An embroidered late 16th-century table carpet giving a lively view of the English countryside with a hunt in progress.

36 'An Assembly, made in the presence of Queen Elizabeth' from Turberville's *The Noble Arte of Venerie* (1575). But for the anachronism, we might call it a royal picnic (note the familiar cold chicken), but 'picnics' as such did not come in until the 18th century. It was probably a distinction without much of a difference. (See also pl. 70, 71)

37 A late 16th-century wedding feast at which actors and musicians provide entertainment. Weddings and funerals have usually been occasions for feasting.

38 Morris dancers by the Thames at Richmond, early 17th century. The importance of Morris dancing in the life of the people was shown by the express approval it received in the *Book of Sports*. It was almost certainly descended from ancient fertility rites and had many parallels elsewhere in Europe but by the 16th century it had developed distinctively English characteristics. It was especially associated with May Day and other spring holidays. Morris dancing survived in a few places until the end of the 19th century. It was discovered by Cecil Sharp in Oxfordshire in 1899, and the Morris dance became one of the chief dances of the folk-dance revival.

39 This drawing of a scene from Act I of *Titus Andronicus* is attributed – probably correctly – to 1595, and if so it may be the only surviving contemporary picture of a scene from Shakespeare as actually played. It shows how the actors were placed and how the producer tried to recreate the costumes of the classical period.

40 From Henry Peacham, *Minerva Brittana* (1612)

The country Swaines, at footeball heere
are seene,
Which each gapes after, for to get a
blow,
The while some one, away runnes with
it cleane,
It meetes another, at the goale below,
Who never stirrd, one catcheth heere a
fall,
And there one's maimd, who never saw
the ball.

41 In *The Art of Archerie* (1634) Gervase Markham stated the case for archery in both peace and war. Perhaps it was to enlist royal support in arresting its decline that he dedicated his treatise to Charles I, who is not known to have been an archer.

THE
ART OF
ARCHERIE.
Shewing how it is most necessary in these times for this
Kingdome, both in Peace and War,
and how it may be done without
charge to the Country, trouble to
the People, or any hinderance
to necessary Occasi-
ons.

ALSO,
Of the Discipline, the Postures,
and whatsoever else is necessarie
for the attayning to the
Art.

LONDON,
Printed by *B. A.* and *T. F.* for B E N:
FISHER, and are to be sold at his Shop,
at the Signe of the *Talbot* without *Alders-*
Gate. 1 6 3 4.

42 'Men very skilful in the art of Pyrotechnic' were to be found in early 17th-century London, and this was one of the 'green men' with clubs charged with squibs and crackers who took part in the displays they organised for 'triumph and recreation'. Later examples of pyrotechnics in popular recreation include the famous displays at Ranelagh (pl. 65) and the Crystal Palace, not to mention Guy Fawkes Day.

43 Isaak Walton and his contemporaries had at their disposal techniques and equipment which were basically the same as today.

THE
Experienc'd
Angler;
or
Angling
Improved.

Sold by Rich Marriott in St Dunstans Church yard
Vaughan sculp.

THE

Experienc'd Angler:

OR

ANGLING
IMPROV'D.

BEING

A general Discourse of Angling;

Imparting many of the aptest wayes
and choicest Experiments for the
taking of most sorts of Fish in
Pond or River.

LONDON:
Printed for *Richard Marriot*, and are to be sold
at his Shop in St. *Dunstans* Church-yard,
Fleet-street. 1662.

44 Country sports and pastimes on the eve of the Civil War, exemplified by the Cotswold Games, which had probably been started under Elizabeth. They acquired a national reputation as a result of their promotion by 'Captain' Robert Dover, who obtained the patronage of James I.

45 The burning of the *Book of Sports* by the public hangman on Cheapside in 1643 on the command of the Long Parliament showed its emotive significance as a symbol of the old order.

46 Royalist propagandists tried to exploit popular resentment against the suppression of Christmas. In this pamphlet (1653) the rejection of old Father Christmas by the Puritans was contrasted with his welcome in a Devonshire village. Here harmless Christmas games like hot cockles were being enjoyed. Some played cards and sang pleasant songs, and the hinds and maidservants and ploughboys danced nimbly. 'They skipped and leaped for joy, singing a carol to the tune of hey.'

47 If not as far back as its legendary foundation by King Bladud in 863 BC, from Roman times Bath was intermittently visited by the sick in search of a cure. Three visits by James I's Queen helped to make it fashionable for invalids, and it began to develop as a pleasure resort before the Civil War. By 1675 it was attracting large numbers of fashionable people whose main purpose was amusement, including evidently swimming and diving. (See also pl. 84)

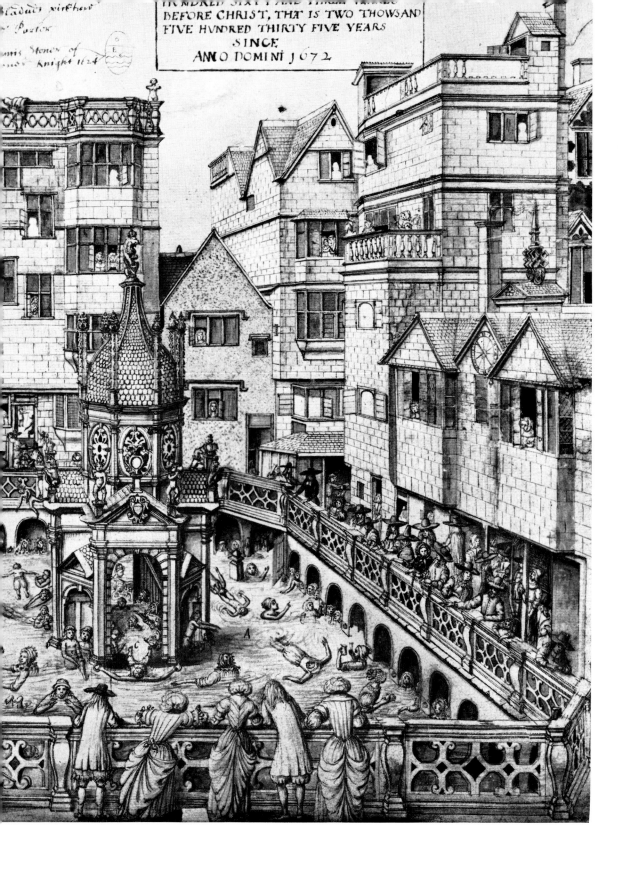

THE COMPLEAT GAMESTER:

48 The five games which Charles Cotton chose for the title page to *The Compleat Gamester* (1674) were: billiards; backgammon; hazard, for long the most popular game among those who played for high stakes; cocking, for which like billiards Cotton had a special affection; and cards, which was suitable for women as well as men.

49 Sir Thomas Parkyns (1664-1741), 'the wrestling baronet' of Bunny Hall, Notts. devoted his main energies to the promotion of Cornish-style wrestling. He was also a runner, a change-ringer and a collector of stone coffins – a reminder of the diversity of human recreations.

50 The earliest known picture of a race-meeting records Charles II's 'last' horse-race before his death in 1685. This was at Dorsett Ferry which was not far from Ascot Heath. (See also pl. 89)

51 'If you would hunt an otter,' wrote Richard Blome in *The Gentleman's Recreation* (1686), 'you must be provided with otter-hounds, and spears.' The sport was known in the Middle Ages, and it still survives, though without the spears.

52 Important advances in shooting had begun by Blome's time. 'It is now the mode,' he said, 'to shoot flying.' But a stalking horse – live or artificial – was a help. To those who used live horses he gave sound advice. 'Let your stalking horse be of the largest size, 'tis no matter how old he be, but he must be well trained for your purpose.'

54 Taking the waters at Tunbridge Wells in the reign of Charles II. Unlike Bath, Tunbridge Wells had no history until the accidental discovery of its springs in 1606, but it had the advantage of greater proximity to London and it quickly became fashionable after the Restoration. In the 18th century it was next in importance to Bath.

55 Remember, John,
    If any ask, to th' Coffee House I'm gone.
By the time of Queen Anne there were about 500 coffee houses in London.

56 At the great frost fair on the Thames in 1683 the many amusements included skating, bull-baiting, horse and coach-racing and puppet-shows. There were also, said John Evelyn, 'tippling and other lewd places, so that it seemed to be a bacchanalian triumph'.

57 Like Southwark Fair and May Fair, the ancient Bartholomew Fair was devoted to amusement in the 18th century. Performing animals, learned pigs and horses, freaks, jugglers, puppet-shows kept up medieval traditions of popular entertainment. The conduct of the crowds troubled the city authorities. The fair was cut down to three days in 1708 but lasted until 1855.

by Hogarth with a similar purpose include 'Marriage à la Mode', 'Gin Lane', 'Beer Street', 'Industry and Idleness', and 'The Four States of Cruelty'.

59 'A Midnight Modern Conversation', by William Hogarth. G. M. Trevelyan found it hard to say whether the men of fashion or the rural gentry were the worse soakers in the 18th century. Women were expected to be more abstemious.

60 Hogarth in a pastoral mood (1738). The scene shows 'the return of a wealthy citizen, his wife and children, from a Sunday afternoon ramble' outside 'a house of entertainment . . . near Sadlers Wells'. The problems of outings with small children have not changed.

61 William Hogarth, 'The Idle Prentice Executed at Tyburn' 1747. '*Le peuple anglais*', wrote a French visitor in 1776, '*naturellement paresseux, ivrogne et brute, est distrait, tantôt par un pendaison, tantôt par une élection, par des fêtes, et par d'abominables combats de boeufs en pleine rue.*' London artisans and apprentices were given holidays to attend the public executions.

62 Scarborough, 1735. The medical fashion for cold-water bathing led logically to the vogue for sea-bathing, just as the drinking of mineral waters was followed by sea-water drinking. As an important spa which was also on the coast, Scarborough was well placed to take advantage of these trends. The first regular sea-bathing season developed at Scarborough, but when the 'rush into the sea' (as Cowper called it) gathered speed in the second half of the 18th century, fashionable people flocked to the South coast which was closer to London.

63 H. Bunbury, 'A Tour to Foreign Parts', arriving at a French inn in the late 18th century. Foreign travel for pleasure began in the quest for culture. The young men who went on the Grand Tour were increasingly followed by older people in search of the cultural centres, watering places, gambling saloons and mountain prospects to be found on the Continent. Many were confirmed in their sense of national superiority but few emulated the gentleman who stayed only one night 'on finding at Calais that he could not have beef steaks well dressed'.

64 Different sections of society appear in this picture (*c.* 1735) of St James's Park and the Mall with Westminster Abbey and the St James's Park canal in the background. Near the centre, with a group of companions, is Frederick Prince of Wales, and a small man wearing the garter seen from the back on the left is probably George II. The promenade – whether in town or at spa or seaside resort – was a characteristic 18th-century amusement: foreigners noted the mixing of classes with surprise.

65 The ball at Ranelagh on the Prince of Wales' birthday in 1759. The famous gardens were opened in 1742 and were closed because of declining support in 1805. Every summer they offered fashionable people 'fêtes, frolics, fireworks, frivolity' (Goldsmith). They were used for breakfast as well as evening parties: except on gala nights only light refreshments were served in the evening.

66 'Fives, Played at the Tennis Court, Leicester Fields' in the late 18th century, but the game is rackets and not fives in the modern sense. Fives as we know it was not clearly differentiated from similar ball games played with bat or hand until the middle of the 19th century. The name probably originated in the five fingers of the hand.

67 Golf near Edinburgh Castle, 1745. The rules prepared by the Honourable Company of Edinburgh Golfers in 1744 were the prototype from which later rules for golf were developed by the Royal and Ancient Club at St Andrews – founded in 1754. Note the use of caddies. (See also pl. 141)

68 A cricket match in Marylebone Fields, 1748. Still in parts truly rural, Marylebone was associated with cricket long before the opening of Thomas Lord's first ground in 1787 and the formation of the famous club in 1788. Note the curved bats, the two-stump wickets, the under-arm bowling, the umpires and the arrangement of the fielders.

69 A meeting of the Hainault Foresters at Fairlop Oak in 1794. The Hainault Foresters, who were formed in 1789, were one of the many archery societies which sprang up after Sir Ashton Lever founded the Toxophilite Society in 1781. The Royal Dukes took an interest, many ladies joined, the picturesque uniforms helped to attract members, and some of the societies paid more attention to the drafting of their dining than their shooting regulations.

70 71 A picnic on Pinnacle Island, one of the Farne Islands, *c.* 1778: above (70) and below stairs (71). Those taking part belonged to a house party, and it is doubtful whether it was a picnic in the original sense of the term as first recorded in England in 1748 – 'a fashionable social entertainment in which each party present contributed a share of the provisions' (Shorter Oxford English Dictionary).

72 Country dancing in the servants' hall, *c.*1775. Local versions of the traditional country dances were kept up in some areas but the English country dance was also the most popular ballroom dance in the 18th century. It was even exported to France where it was known as the Contredanse Anglaise at the Court of Louis XIV.

73 Highland dance in 1782, soon after the ban on wearing the kilt was raised. This was the real thing, but Scottish dancing also had a vogue in England in the late 18th and early 19th centuries. It was no doubt connected with the romantic interest in Scotland stimulated by the popularity of Sir Walter Scott's poems and novels. French interest in Scotland and Scottish music had already produced the Écossaise. The Schottische was invented in Germany in the middle of the 19th century.

74 James Gillray, 'Tales of Wonder (dedicated to Monk Lewis)', 1802. From primeval ghost stories to horror films, rugger scrums and Alpine ascents, what Dorothy Sayers called the art of selftormenting has made a curious and important contribution to recreation. Matthew Gregory Lewis's *The Monk* (1796) was one of the most extravagant and shocking of the late 18th-century novels of terror. 'A mere mess and blotch of murder, outrage, *diablerie* and indecency,' said the literary critic George Saintsbury.

75 James Gillray, 'Blowing up the Pic Nics-or Harlequin quixote attacking the puppets', 1802. For the private theatricals of the Pic Nic Society a small theatre was erected at the Tottenham Street concert rooms. Sheridan announced his determination to oppose the society as an infringement of the monopoly of the theatre. The engraving shows Sheridan leading the forces of the professionals against the amateurs. An outcry prophesying divine judgement was also caused because rehearsals had been held on a Sunday.

76 James Gillray, 'La Walse, le bon genre', 1810. Though of German origin the modern waltz dates from the close-holding French version which shocked much of Europe and became fashionable here after being danced by the Tsar at Almack's in 1815. *The Times* noted 'with pain' in 1816 that 'the indecent foreign dance called the waltz' had been introduced at the English Court. Byron said of a waltzing couple that they looked like two cockchafers 'spitted on the same bodkin'.

77 The unco-ordinated activity of the morning promenade upon the cliff at Brighton (Gillray, 1806) contrasted with the orderly social life of the spas. In the same year Lady Jerningham compared the 'quiet, pleasant sociable intercourse' of Tunbridge Wells with 'this great staring, bustling, unsocial Brighton'.

78 T. Rowlandson, 'Mr. H. Angelo's fencing academy', 1791. The fencing academy founded by Domenico Angelo in 1763 was a well-known London institution until its closure in 1897. Its fame was mainly due to Domenico's son Harry who attracted fashionable support in the 1780s by arranging matches between visiting French professors and resident masters. In view of the competition from pugilism he later shared his rooms in Bond Street with the school of pugilism run by 'Gentleman' John Jackson.

79 Backgammon, according to Strutt, was 'not often practised' by 1801 but it had still been popular in the early 18th century, especially with the clergy. 'In what esteem are you with the vicar of the parish,' Jonathan Swift asked a friend, 'can you play with him at backgammon?' Passions sometimes ran high. Hazlitt wrote in 1822 of a losing player who threw the board out of the window.

84 'The Comforts of Bath. A concert,' from Rowlandson's illustrations to Christopher Anstey's *New Bath Guide* (1798). As Anstey said: 'I'm certain none of Hogarth's sketches, e'er formed a set of stranger wretches.'

85 The comforts of Scarborough – the library as seen by Rowlandson in 1813. By this time there were circulating libraries in most towns. 'All our ladies read now,' Samuel Johnson had said in 1778.

86 The discomforts of Scarborough – the departure as seen by Rowlandson in 1813.

87 After being beaten in 33 rounds in 1810, the American negro Tom Molineaux challenged Tom Cribb, the champion of England, to a second fight in 1811. National pride was involved, and 20,000 spectators attended the fight in Leicestershire; a quarter of them, it was estimated, belonged to the upper classes. Cribb almost slaughtered Molineaux in 20 minutes. His patron, Captain Barclay, who was also a famous pedestrian, won £10,000 on the fight.

88 Johnson's Pedestrian Hobby-horse Riding School, 1819. The hobbyhorse was introduced into England from France in 1818 and acquired the nickname 'dandy-horse' because of its vogue among people of fashion including the Prince Regent. It was a toy with no lasting significance. The first true bicycle was made in Scotland in 1840, and cycling began to be popular after the invention of the 'vélocipède' in France in the 1860s. The first successful safety bicycle was the Rover model of 1885. (See also pl. 114, 123)

89 Epsom races, 1821. Regular meetings at Epsom seem to have begun in 1730, and the Derby was instituted in 1780. By 1830 it was the major event in the racing year. As will be seen, there was much more to a race-meeting than just watching the races. (See also pl. 132)

90 Like 95-97 this illustration is taken from Henry Alken's *British Sports* (1821), in which he expressed his hatred of cruelty to animals as well as his love of sport. 'The bull-fights of Spain and Portugal are equally atrocious,' he said, 'but far more dangerous and manly than English bull-baits.' Bull-baiting had already ceased to be respectable in England, and was fast dying out.

91 Whist – here being played in 1821 – is mentioned as 'whisk' in 1621, and under its present name soon after the Restoration. Modern whist evolved in the 18th century, and it was probably the most widely played of card games until the rise of auction bridge. Bridge, auction bridge and contract bridge were in logical as well as historical succession from whist as it was developed on scientific lines by Cavendish in the second half of the 19th century.

92 At a masquerade supper in 1821. Like children, men and women at all periods have enjoyed dressing up. The Saturnalia, medieval mumming, the Jacobean masque, the masquerades at Ranelagh, the charade and the fancy dress ball are all in the same tradition.

93 'The great actor Mr Punch', 1825. The Italian character, Punchinello, quickly abbreviated to Punch, first appeared in English puppet-shows after the Restoration. As a glove-puppet street show 'Punch and Judy' dates from the late 18th century: Punch's wife was originally called Joan and why she changed her name is unknown. Note that the audience is almost wholly adult.

94 A 'bowling alley', 1825, but we should call it a green. Bowls was in decline by the early 19th century, and the revival which began in Scotland was not fully under way in England until the 1900s. (See also pl. 18, 130)

95 Large sums were wagered on the shooting of pigeons released from traps and it was justified on the ground that it gave every participant an equal chance. Despite its cruelty it grew in popularity during the 19th century: Hurlingham had become a fashionable centre by the 1870s. Bills to suppress the sport failed to pass in 1883 and 1884, and – almost incredibly – it was not banned until 1921.

96 Hawking never entirely died out, and it had a minor revival in the early 19th century. Like the revival of archery and attempts later to reestablish the tournament this probably reflected romantic interest in the Middle Ages.

97 By the 1820s there was no doubt except among enthusiasts for hare-hunting about the pre-eminence which fox-hunting had established over other forms of hunting. It did not yet have to face the menace of the railway which led Robert Surtees to predict that 'in a few years, hunting in England will be mere matter of history'. In fact it survived worse dangers – political and social revolution, barbed wire, the motor-car, the tractor, and humanitarian criticism.

98 'Hunting supper, the Toast.' Fox-hunting derived much of its strength from the cohesion it gave to country life by bringing people together at hunt suppers and hunt balls as well as at meets. No women were present at this hunt supper.

99 By the beginning of the 19th century little remained of the former harvest home customs except the harvest supper, sometimes preceded by a procession like this. Rowlandson (1823).

100 Posterity is indebted to antiquarians such as William Hone who recorded dying holiday customs before it was too late. Traces of the customs connected with Plough Monday, the Monday after Twelfth Day, persisted in a few places as late as the 1870s.

101 Nor and spell – or, as Strutt called it, 'Northern-spell' – was still played in the North in the early 19th century. Strutt thought it possessed little variety, and was 'by no means so amusing to the bystander as cricket or trap-ball'. The game had affinities to golf: the object was to hit the ball as far as possible in a given number of strokes.

102 Newcastle pitmen playing at quoits in 1843. Many of the old pastimes survived longest in the closed mining and agricultural communities.

103 An Oxford 'bottle party', 1825. University students have traditionally been allowed a licence not accorded to most other young men and wholly withheld from young women until the 1920s. Of medieval English students in Paris it was said that they ate too much and drank too much and were addicted to whoring but otherwise there was nothing particularly wrong with them.

104 'The gin shop rising like a palace', a witness told a Parliamentary Committee in 1834, 'absorbs the wealth and the health and the life of the labouring class.' George Cruikshank was an advocate of total abstinence, and it was to further the cause of temperance that he published *The Drunkard's Children* (1848) in which this famous engraving 'The Gin Shop' appeared.

105 Christmas pantomime, 1837. In its modern English form the pantomime goes back to the harlequinade which was invented by John Rich in 1717. For more than a century it was a dumb show not specifically associated with Christmas but by the 1830s words had been added and it was increasingly confined to the Christmas season. By the 20th century it had become a revue with a steretotyped framework, lightly based on traditional children's stories and with stock characters such as a male dame and a female principal boy. There were 100 Christmas pantomimes in 1933 and nearly 200 in 1948.

106 George Cruikshank sums up Christmas food. With its emphasis on the family and neighbourliness, the Victorian Christmas evolved as a reaction against the materialism of what had become a festival primarily concerned with food and drink.

107 Albert Smith's 'Ascent of Mont Blanc' drew new crowds to the Egyptian Hall after he added 'accessories in themselves realities' in 1852. They included a full-size exterior of a Swiss chalet, an Alpine pool with live fish, chamois skins, knapsacks and vintage baskets.

108 The famous Oxford Music Hall in 1861, the year of its opening by Charles Morton, the 'Father of the Halls'. The early music-halls of the 1840s and 1850s had sprung up in working class areas, and Morton was the first to foresee the possibilities of a West End clientèle among 'men about town' and the 'sporting fraternity'.

109 Cruikshank speculates on the future of 'cheap excursion trains' in 1850. 'Of course we shall have a Railway to Grand Cairo – the London and Great Desert Direct,' and the desert sands will become 'as much frequented as those of Ramsgate.'

110 'Weston sands', 1864. 'Every year a month or so by the sea, sands and donkey rides, sea anemones, bathing, blackberries and cream.' (G. Lowes Dickinson, looking back to his holidays as a child in the 1860s.)

111 Hockey, 1864. As it developed in the mid-Victorian public schools hockey was at first disorganised and violent: like football it had to be humanised and regulated before it took its place in the modern repertoire of team-games. As we now know it, it dates from the middle 1870s. The Hockey Association was founded in 1886.

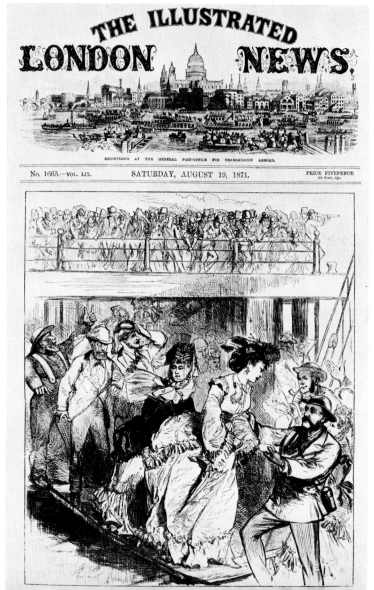

112 Margate jetty on 'the Statute Holiday' (alias August Bank Holiday), 1871. Lubbock's hope that the new bank holidays would become general holidays was quickly fulfilled. There were amazing scenes at the London railway stations and steamboat piers on the first August Bank Holiday in 1871, and the Margate boats arrived after they were due to return. (See also pl. 124)

113 Inter-university hurdling in 1871. A 140-yard hurdle race – the standard distance is now 120 yards – was included in an early athletic sports meeting organized by Exeter College, Oxford, in 1850. The first Oxford and Cambridge sports were held in 1864.

114 The start of the bicycling race from Bath to London in 1874. This now unusual method was used to choose the captain and 'sub-captain' of the Middlesex Bicycle Club. With a speed of more than 10 m.p.h. inclusive of stoppages, the winner broke not only the cycling but the stage-coach record.

115 In 1877 the Oxford and Cambridge boat race ended in the only dead heat on record. First rowed at Henley in 1829, it became annual in 1856. By the 1870s it was a popular armchair sport – recorded here in the inimitable *Illustrated London News*.

116 Technology was called in to promote a sport for which the English climate was not well suited. The first artificial ice rink was built in Chelsea in 1876; it had a gallery for spectators and an orchestra, and was open to the noblemen and gentlemen who were subscribers. But there were technical problems – of avoiding excessive mist and dampness – which were not yet solved.

117 Lawn tennis could be played by both sexes and at most ages and levels of skill. It also made a pleasant social occasion – even for the grandmother who read her newspaper while she watched. It mattered little if she did not understand what the caption to George du Maurier's cartoon called the 'barbarous technicalities', including such mysteries as 'shooting' and 'hanging' in serving. This was 1882.

118 George du Maurier's drawings brilliantly conveyed the spirit of London social life in the last quarter of the 19th century. *Mutatis mutandis* this musical at home – entitled 'Killing two birds with one stone' – was representative of similar occasions at other social levels. (See also pl. 134)

119 The formal dinner-party with its strict protocol, its complex ritual and its prescribed costume was a major Victorian and Edwardian social institution. The upper middle classes took themselves and their pleasures seriously, and set high standards of consumption, hospitality and ceremony. This is a du Maurier cartoon of 1882.

120 A doctor's family playing croquet in 1865: the paterfamilias is seated on the right. But croquet soon got into the hands of the experts. By adding to its complexity they almost killed it as a game for the average player.

121 Gipsies with a dancing bear, *c*.1900. Of the street entertainers who flourished in the Victorian and Edwardian periods few survived the First World War. By the 1960s practically none remained except musicians, buskers and pavement artists.

122 Late Victorian seaside scene. As a song of the 1880's said:
'Oh, I love to sit a-gyzing on the boundless blue horizing,
When the scorching sun is blyzing down on sands, and ships, and sea!
And to watch the busy figgers of the happy little diggers.'

123 The cycling boom of the 1890s affected all ages and all classes.

124 August Bank Holiday on Hampstead Heath, *c*.1890. Neither puritanism nor poverty inhibited the spontaneous gaiety with which Londoners enjoyed themselves at the fairs held at Hampstead Heath and other open spaces on the summer bank-holidays. The Heath had been saved for the public in two stages during the 1860s and 1880s.

125 Cockney pearly kings, early 20th century.

126 Old women's outing at Loughton, 1908. For purposes like this the portability of the gramophone was a great advantage, but like the transistor radio in the 1960s it was sometimes a nuisance to other people.

127 Regent's Park Zoo, *c.*1890. The Zoological Gardens in Regent's Park had been opened by the Zoological Society in 1828, and they took over the animals from the royal collection at the Tower which had been a great attraction to Londoners since the Middle Ages. The numbers visiting the new Zoo grew from about 200,000 a year at first to about 2 million a century later.

128 129 A camera club at work and refreshing itself in the 1890s. Like the gramophone, the camera harnessed technology to art and recreation. For ordinary people with less time and enthusiasm than these, the story of amateur photography began with the mass production of ready-made dry plates in 1878. The veriest tyro could use the Kodak cameras and celluloid roll-films which were introduced from America in the late 1880s, and printing and developing services did the processing for him.

130 Bowls, *c.*1890s. After nearly dying out as a public-house game (pl. 94) bowls revived in the public parks which were provided under Victorian legislation. The 'flat' version prevailed in Scotland and the South, but the crown green game – with rougher greens rising to the centre – was also popular in the North.

131 In 1906 the Chairman of the London County Council performed the dedication ceremony of Hainault Forest, one of the larger open spaces acquired by the Council for popular recreation outside the county boundaries.

132 The Prince of Wales leading in Persimmon after winning the Derby in 1896.

133 The Henley Regatta began in 1839, became 'Royal' after the Prince Consort's visit in 1851, and as a social as well as a sporting event was at its height between 1887 and 1914. This picture was taken in 1908.

134 'The piano thumpers', 1908. An Edwardian version of the musical evening (see pl. 118). The gramophone foreshadowed a new era in musical entertainment at home (see pl. 143).

135 Amateur drama as well as amateur music. The Camel Play actors at Queen Camel, Somerset, 1912.

136 A bioscope show at Melford Fair in Suffolk, *c.*1908. Though in a traditional fairground setting, the programmes and the publicity methods anticipated the future.

137 May Day celebrations, Stratford-on-Avon, 1914. The May Queen and the maypole were drawn by a team of oxen. Revivals of obsolete customs were always self-conscious and almost always ephemeral.

138 The Scottish Motor Trials, 1906, the stop at Inverarjy. Road racing was forbidden in Britain but the industry organized road reliability trials in which cars were tested by professionals and amateurs under difficult conditions within the statutory speed limits.

139 The start of a relay race at Brooklands in 1909. Motor racing is almost as old as the motor car – a road race in France was won at 15m.p.h. in 1894 – but its development in Britain was held up because of the ban on using the roads for racing. With the opening of Brooklands in 1907 Britain had as fine a track as any in the world.

140 A Manchester trade picnic, 1912, with the party at Stratford-on-Avon. Note the charabancs – the prototypes of the motor-coach. There had long been an organised Shakespeare industry at Stratford.

141 The Ladies' golf championship at Sandwich, 1922. At golf and lawn tennis the standards of the best women players were not much inferior to those of the best men. At most other sports men outclassed women. At swimming, skating and riding women fully held their own.

142 Dancing the tango in 1925. The tango, which was ultimately of African negro origin, came to Europe from the Argentine *via* the United States. It made a sensational impact upon London in 1912. By the 1920s other American dances like the Charleston had overtaken its power to shock the public.

143 2LO's 'Invisible Band' on the air, 1923. The possibilities of wireless as a medium of musical entertainment were first brought home to the British public by a broadcast by Melba in 1920. 'Art and science joined hands', commented the *Daily Mail*, 'in a wonderful half-hour.'

144 Cocktail party, 1930, 'the kind one goes to' rather than 'the kind one reads about'. Gin-based and transatlantic, for some people the cocktail symbolized the hectic feverishness of the post-war years. Wimbledon and Purley preferred sherry.

145 'Sunday at Llanculgwn', 1937. Sabbatarianism persisted longest in Wales and Scotland. Note the characteristic attire of the hikers of the 1930s.

146 'Open-air sports', as seen by Pont in 1938. The armchair sportsman is ready with his newspaper to check the football results from the loudspeaker on the sitting-room table.

147 A keep-fit class at Butlin's holiday camp at Filey in 1946. For an inclusive charge the larger holiday camps offered a wide range of activities suitable for all ages and most tastes, except those of the totally unsociable or misanthropic.

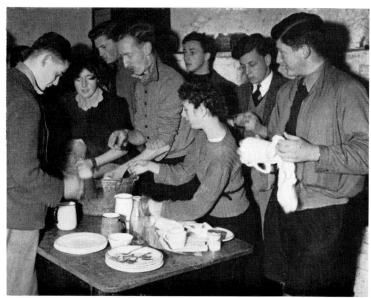

148 Grasmere Youth Hostel, late 1940s. Self-help was expected of the youth hosteller: the overnight charge was only a shilling before the Second World War.

149 Popular entertainment during the Second World War. Greyhounds ready for the start of a race at the White City, with the attendants in national head-gear, and the tote winnings on an earlier race in the background.

150 Open air concert at Kenwood, Hampstead Heath, in the 1960s. Kenwood House and grounds were acquired by the London County Council in the 1920s.

151 Scenes like that depicted in L.S. Lowry's painting 'Going to the match' are still typical of Saturday afternoons in Northern industrial areas, notwithstanding the falling off of attendances at football matches owing to television and other causes. The preponderance of males is characteristic. It is Bolton Wanderers ground.

152 The Grand Match, or North v. South curling contest, on the Lake of Monteith, Perthshire, in 1963. This was only the second time since 1935 that ice conditions enabled it to be held. 900 a side took part: 'the distillers did pretty well, too,' reported the *Observer*. Curling is especially identified with Scotland, and the Royal Caledonian Curling Club is recognised internationally as the regulating body.

153 Ten-pin bowling at Croydon, 1960s. The cinema interests turned to the promotion of ten-pin bowling and bingo (pl. 154) in order to offset the decline in cinema attendances because of television. Ten-pin bowling is a mechanised and commercialised American form of nine-pins.

154 Bingo at Morden, in the 1960s. A boom in bingo followed the Betting and Gaming Act of 1960. The Churches' Council on Gambling estimated that the turnover was £35 million in 1965. During the same year a jackpot prize of over £2000 was won at the Empire Pool, Wembley, in the biggest bingo game ever held under one roof. Bingo is a new name for what was formerly known as lotto or housey-housey: it seems to have been taken from a version of dominoes based on bezique.

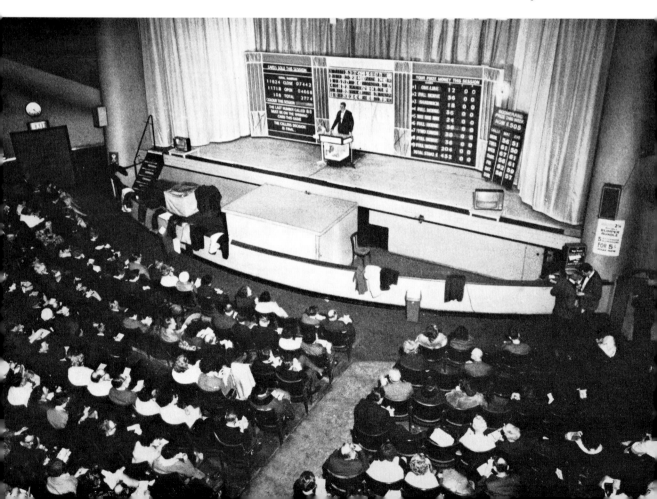

155 A pub scene of 1967: 10.28 p.m. or just before the usual closing time. Most of the drinkers are perpendicular, all are male, beer is the staple drink, and they are watching soccer on TV. Live telecasts of Cup and League matches (except the Cup Final as a national event) were forbidden by the Football Association and the Football League because of the threat to actual attendances.

156 'A nation of gardeners?' It was estimated in the 1960s that to one gardener out of three gardening was a disagreeable chore.

" ... AND THEN, BEYOND THE LAWNS, A LILY POOL WITH FOUNTAINS
AND A ROSE PERGOLA LEADING TO A RUSTIC SUMMER HOUSE .... "

157 Trecco Bay caravan site at Porthcawl, Glamorgan, in the 1960s. In the middle 1960s about 5 million people a year spent their holidays in caravans or tents out of over 30 million who took holidays away from home. 5-6 million attended cinemas every week, about the same number went to dance halls, 1 million played golf, 2 million fished, 2 million attended evening classes, 7 million were keen gardeners, and between 40 and 50 million watched television. Over £1000 million was spent on alcoholic drink, and much the same (in gross terms) on gambling. Towards a civilization of leisure?

INDEX

The figures in italics refer to illustrations and captions